*"I have walked the long road and
kept to my journey...I have lost and found myself
in every rock, field and tree. I know what I am and
what I imagine. I know shadow and light, and I
have never been satisfied with shelter and bread
when the great was left unattained."*

—Normandi Ellis, *Awakening Osiris*

BLUE LOTUS BOOKS

ISBN 979-8-218-10008-7

WAKING
THE
TEMPLES

CALLAN KANE

ACKNOWLEDGEMENTS

Two people in particular made this book possible. My beloved daughter Avalon, whose graphic design, editing, and proofreading were invaluable. Her computer expertise and emotional support were even more critical to the book's publication.

To my best friend in life and even before birth— my twin sister Dr. Mary Donohue—thank you for your professional editing, honest feedback, limitless confidence in my abilities, and sincere enjoyment of *Waking the Temples*!

Though names have been changed to protect their privacy, I am forever grateful to the people known in the memoir as Michael and Shani. You made my trip to Egypt exceed my wildest expectations. In your expert care and enlightened company I was safe, educated, entertained, and allowed to follow my own sacred path to Egypt's immortal magic.

To my travel companion and treasured friend Sara: Thank you for your willingness to accompany me on my adventures. Your positive attitude, flexibility, sense of humor, open-mindedness, and generosity are a priceless gift. The unexpected upgrade to first class over the pond was an epic surprise!

And of course to the people of Egypt, who welcomed me at every turn, went out of their way to ensure my safety, and opened their temples and their hearts.
Shukren!

For

Hathor

&

Horus

I arrived like a priestess in leopard skin.

I sailed the Nile, collecting the temples' secrets
like carnelian beads on a necklace of gold.

I saw myself with the eyes of a falcon and
burned frankincense and myrrh on the altar of my becoming.

Along the way my heart danced red stones into the sand,
making a path for the magic to find me.

When it did, I lay my head in its lap like a child.
Upon arising, I no longer needed the gown of a goddess.

I am content to be my own simple vessel,
honored to pour for you the wine of remembering.

—Callan Kane

ITINERARY

PART 1: LOWER EGYPT

GIZA

SAQQARA

Dahshur

PART II: UPPER EGYPT

DENDERA

ANCIENT THEBES

THE NILE RIVER

ASWAN

PART III:
THE GREAT PYRAMID

PART I:

LOWER EGYPT

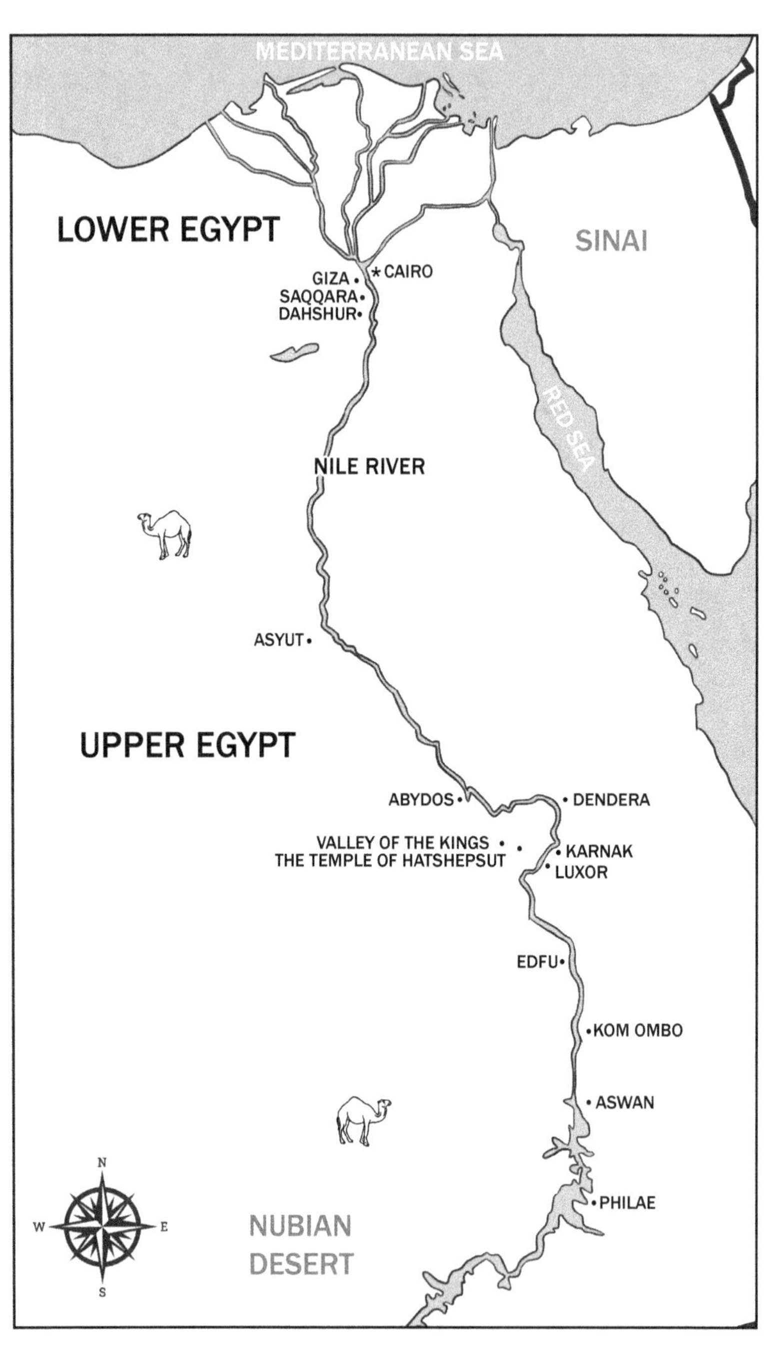

MEDITERRANEAN SEA
LOWER EGYPT
SINAI
GIZA
SAQQARA
DAHSHUR
CAIRO
RED SEA
NILE RIVER
ASYUT
UPPER EGYPT
ABYDOS
DENDERA
VALLEY OF THE KINGS
THE TEMPLE OF HATSHEPSUT
KARNAK
LUXOR
EDFU
KOM OMBO
ASWAN
PHILAE
N
W
E
S
NUBIAN
DESERT

Chapter 1

THE
VALLEY TEMPLE

I'm leaning up against a 200-ton, expertly worked granite pillar, gazing up past the Valley Temple architraves to where luscious white clouds are seducing Ra. The shadows of their union remove his searing burn from my exposed forearms and I look at my watch to see what hour of Egyptian morning is producing this kind of heat. My fellow tourists are flattened like moths against the towering temple walls, fanning themselves and reapplying sunscreen. Around us, sixteen gigantic, square monolithic columns rise in perfect, orderly rows. Upon the towering pillars, shockingly large rectangular stones are balanced. The edges match so perfectly as to appear machined. It's an environment of extreme symmetry, stark and handsome. But where are the hieroglyphs and the gods?

I have been dreaming of Egyptian hieroglyphs since I was a child. In my early twenties I even considered becoming an archaeologist. Then wonderful life came calling and like a piece on a board game, I found myself counting the steps toward new goals and landing in some unexpected spaces. Eventually, I folded up the game board and closed the box-top and there she was: Egypt. She had been there the whole time, patiently waiting. It was time to go.

I knew exactly the version of myself that would visit Egypt. She would be professionally rooted, maybe even a tiny bit famous. She would be the wife of a charming, spiritually-aware man. She would have a healthy bank account and a clear path forward toward her own life goals. How incredible to finally be here in Egypt, in this mind-blowing temple next to the actual, real Sphinx. With none. Of. The. Above.

Oh, I've had the ego-satisfying suffixes before: Magazine Editor, Wife, Successful Entrepreneur. It's just that when I realize I've created something really good but not quite the target my soul is aiming for, I feel compelled to let it go. Luckily, I've got more arrows in my quiver and a confident heart. I do envy the sustained relationships and balanced finances of a road consistently traveled but my soul seeks an immortal treasure, and the temple is within.

That's a hard circle to square with husbands. I have been married and divorced twice. When my first husband left me and our baby girl with special needs I was devastated. I remember looking at the sky above the Santa Barbara foothills and watching a red-tailed hawk soaring. Emotionally crushed but defiant, I decreed the hawks would be my husband and I would never be lonely again. That actually worked out pretty well.

My beloved daughter and I made a fresh start up north, where I was able to purchase a house on two acres in the juniper and sagebrush desert of Central Oregon. I got a good job in marketing and for the next ten years I trained and hunted with hawks and falcons in the chaparral around my property. It was the Oregon Department of Fish & Wildlife who bestowed my title for this stage of life: Master Falconer. That's how I met my second husband.

I was married to my second husband when I achieved another lifelong dream: publishing a magazine. It was incredibly challenging, fun, creative, and another decade under the bridge. Mark and I will always be family, but we weren't meant to be a couple until death do us part. I sold the magazine a few years too late but squeaked out debt free and with just enough money to get in some good trouble with an old flame: Egypt.

Like a charismatic movie star, Egypt's intensity and allure are only fully understood in the flesh. And in the stones. But really, where the hell are the hieroglyphs?

It turns out the Valley Temple, along with its Giza Plateau neighbors the Sphinx and the Pyramids, are very different from the monuments of Dynastic Egypt. These older, elegant sites feature precise megalithic building techniques that can't be reproduced today, and certainly not by the bronze age tools and wood rollers they are traditionally attributed to.

Is it possible the temple I'm standing in was here

before the great flood of the Younger Dryas? The cataclysms that tormented Earth between 12,800 and 11,500 years ago are immortalized in biblical stories and indigenous lore alike. Stone cannot be carbon dated, so the age of the world's mysterious megalithic structures must be painstakingly reconstructed by ancient documents, stele (upright stone slabs carved with inscriptions), oral history, and myths. Fortunately, world-wide accounts from diverse and far flung cultures converge to tell the same story: a beneficent human-like species with magical powers helped restart civilization after the great flood. Recently, scientists, geologists, and astronomers have concluded that the ubiquitous flood "myths" are true. During the Younger Dryas, Earth suffered unspeakable destruction by way of multiple comet and meteor strikes, followed by the infamous worldwide deluge. Now that the story of the flood has been proven, what of the contemporaneous accounts of human-like 'gods.'

My palms flatten against a red granite monolith who must wonder who the tiny creature is that clings to his shins. This stone was standing here when Jesus was born and died. Buddha and Jeanne d'Arc were bright stars that flared and vanished in his eternal sky. Beyond the mighty gatekeeper, the cyclopean stones of the temple walls are "wrapped" into ninety-degree corners. It's as if the stone was softened somehow, before being shaped and rehardened into this "impossible" architecture. This type of construction is almost identical to the building styles of Stonehenge, Ancient Peru, and Baalbek, Lebanon. Like enigmatic structures the world over, the oldest Egyptian monuments feature multi-ton masonry blocks fitted together without any mortar and with such precision that even today, a piece of paper cannot be inserted between them. It seems like ancient sorcery. And that's exactly what the ancient stories describe.

Egyptian history is replete with tales of human-like gods who defied the laws of physics. These primordial creator gods—called *neters*—were highly advanced beings who possessed the ability to bend the laws of nature to their wills. They were also considered to *be* the laws themselves, quantum personalities that permeate all matter. It was a time when magical spells could lift a megalithic stone into the air or restore a blinded eye. High Priests and Priestesses could see the future and the past. Stones and statues could communicate after being imbued with the energy of a god or goddess. Temples were "alive," animated by invisible quantum geometries and built with carefully selected stones chosen for their ability to affect human tissue and brain chemistry. The sun, moon, and stars were the heavenly bodies of the neters Ra, Thoth, and Nut.

The fertile black lands bordering the Nile River were historically called *Khem* or *Khemet,* a place where science, spirituality and magic entwined like sacred, inseparable serpents around the staff of life. Our modern word Alchemy is derived from *al-Khem*, or "from Egypt."

The ancient Egyptians believed everything, from a star to a person to a temple was netered. If a human being could achieve a compatible vibratory signature, a sympathetic resonance, then any form of consciousness could be known and intimately related to. Maybe it still can.

✳✳✳

Ra's heat once again falls unveiled upon my body and I glance up to see the lovers have parted ways. Although we entered this below ground, open-air temple from a desiccated wooden ramp on the Giza Plateau, the structure originally stood at ground level. Far back on Egypt's golden timeline, the Nile flowed next to the Valley Temple whose quay welcomed the celestial *barques* (boats) of the gods themselves.

I'm imagining the river's cool waters lapping luxuriously against a warm stone dock. Deep green date palms, lush vegetation, and fragrant flowers would have greeted visitors stepping from their boats and barques onto the temple floor paved in polished alabaster. Even now, many thousands of years later, I can see the original alabaster floor, stretching the entire length of the temple. Examining the pale translucent stones beneath my sneakers reveals their resilient beauty; the huge pavers are worn and dimmed, but still easily recognizable.

Alabaster is a stone of calmness, tranquility and peace. It is said to balance and heal the human nervous system as well as facilitate healthy energy flow to the sexual and creative chakras. What an enchanting way to arrive in the land of Khem.

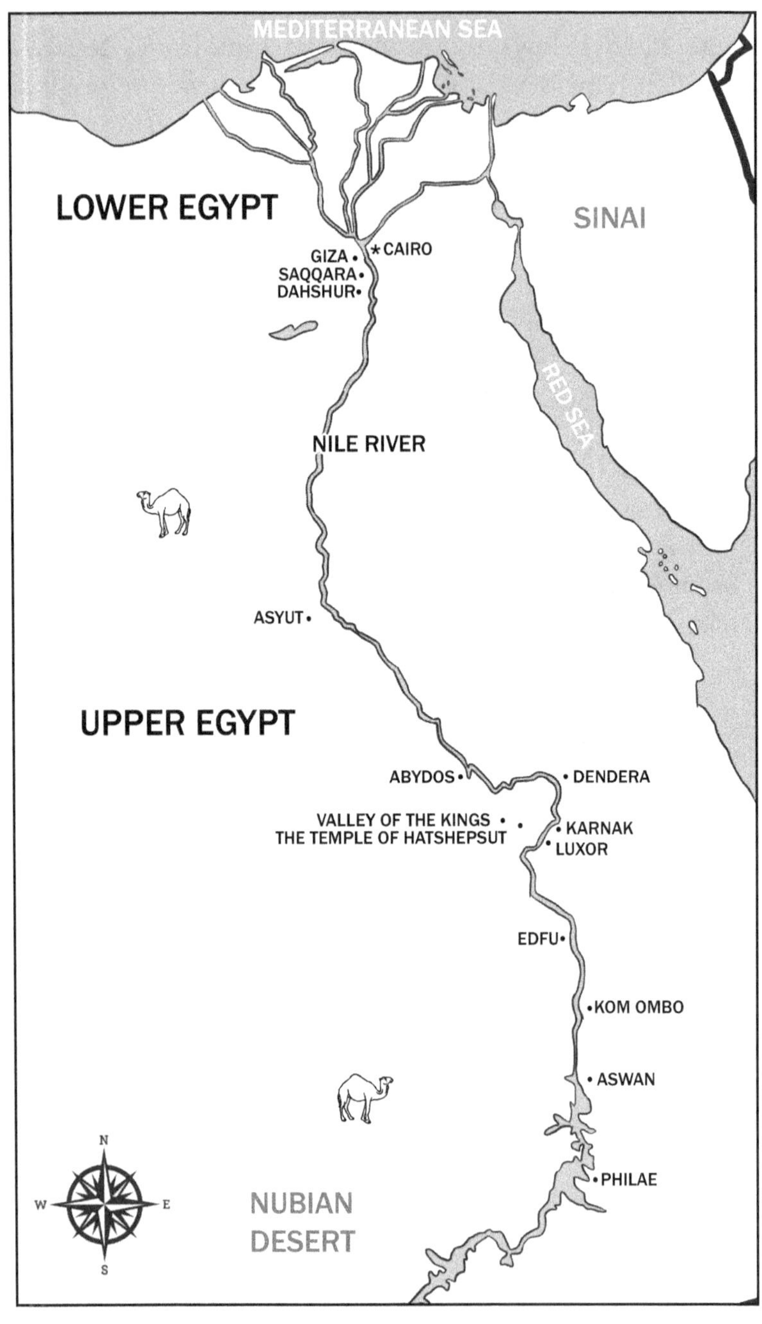

MEDITERRANEAN SEA
LOWER EGYPT
SINAI
GIZA
SAQQARA
DAHSHUR
CAIRO
RED SEA
NILE RIVER
ASYUT
UPPER EGYPT
ABYDOS
DENDERA
VALLEY OF THE KINGS
THE TEMPLE OF HATSHEPSUT
KARNAK
LUXOR
EDFU
KOM OMBO
ASWAN
PHILAE
N
W
E
S
NUBIAN
DESERT

Chapter 2

THE SPHINX

Staring at the Great Sphinx, I'm trying to reconcile a lifetime of photographs and documentaries with this familiar face before my eyes. Like the pyramids, The Sphinx is so much larger than expected, and feels undeniably ancient. It's a strange, haunting perception that isn't conveyed through photographs or video. Archeoastronomers—researchers who study the precession of the equinoxes to correlate temples and monuments with their original astrological alignments— have discovered that 10,500 years ago on the spring equinox, the Sphinx of Giza would have been looking directly at Leo, its namesake constellation, rising on the Egyptian horizon. Today, the Sphinx gazes directly at a Pizza Hut.

In the 1990s, Dr. Robert Schoch, a respected geologist and world-renowned expert on rock weathering, traveled to Egypt to examine the erosion patterns on the Sphinx. His professional opinion: The rivulets on the Sphinx's hindquarters are not consistent with weathering by flooding or wind, they are a result of precipitation. Incredibly, the rainfall amounts needed to create these patterns have not been experienced in this region for at least 20,000 years. This begs the question: Was the Sphinx carved to mirror the constellation Leo in the sky 10,500 years ago, or is this monument even older? Could the Sphinx have been created for the previous 26,000-year processional cycle? That would mean the Sphinx is 36,000 years old!

Skeptics may scoff, yet in the last decade technology has been developed that reveals Earth is covered with previously unknown, non-natural structures. Pyramids, temple complexes and vast civilizations lie under our planet's jungles and deserts. Megalithic citadels are submerged at the bottom of our oceans. Magnificent ancient statues have been pulled from the deep sea. Some of these artifacts may be more than inert stone ruins—they may be long-lost technology.

I'm traveling in Egypt with my friend Sara, who I met in belly dance class and instantly liked. We've gone on several trips together and discovered an easy compatibility. Sara lost her husband a few years ago and has become an avid world traveler. When I announced I was booking a trip to Egypt led by accomplished sacred sites expert Michael Santos, she didn't think twice.

Ascending the path beyond the rear of the Sphinx, Sara and I discover a tall chain link fence with an open gate that leads to a wide, sloping sandstone trail, above which looms the Pyramid of Khafre (Chephren in Greek). This is the second largest pyramid on the plateau, the middle monument making up the three famous Giza Pyramids. A remnant of the tura limestone casing stones which once sheathed the entire structure still cling to its apex. Squinting into the sun's glare I try to imagine the pyramid in ancient times, covered with its original polished white shell, but movement in my peripheral vision demands my attention. Turning to the left, I see Sara slowly lowering herself to sit on a nearby rock. I walk back to where she is pouring water on her wrists and then patting a wet palm on the back of her neck.

"Are you OK?"

"It's the heat," she says, "or maybe the energy coming off this pyramid. I don't think I can go any closer. I'm feeling a little nauseated."

"Oh no," I remove my backpack and search the inside pockets until I find one of the single-serving electrolyte powder packets I've brought. "Here, put this in your water. You might be getting heat exhaustion."

I feel drawn to the towering pyramid like a magnet, but I turn my back on the captivating monument and move to sit down beside my friend. I can't leave Sara here if she's in any kind of trouble.

"I'll be OK," Sara says, swirling the lemon-flavored powder around in her water bottle. "Look," she points down the way we just came, down toward the Sphinx. "There's Michael and some other people from our group coming this way. I'll be fine. I just can't get any closer to that thing right now. I'll wait here for you. You go ahead. This is why you came."

I do see several people from our group approaching. They're still pretty far away but well within rescue distance should Sara need it. The other tourists milling about offer an additional safety net.

"Okay," I hand her my extra water bottle. "Take this in case you need it."

"Thank you. I'll be fine," she insists, accepting the water. I walk away but look back after a few yards. Sara is adjusting her sun hat and stretching out her legs. She looks alright.

***

Walking alone up the wide, gravel causeway behind the Sphinx to the base of the second-largest pyramid in Egypt is surreal. But I'm not really alone. There are camel wranglers touting rides, the bellies of their beasts rocking by me at eye level, dangling colorful, oversized tassels from their girths. Sun-hatted tourists and hijab'd locals pose for selfies as grinning young men shout souvenirs for sale. Two lean Arabian horses gallop by at a dead run. Their riders sit bareback with Keffiyeh scarves bouncing round their shoulders. The horses' hard hoofbeats drum rhythmically away on the blonde rock as a hot breeze blows against my neck. The perspiration on my skin is gone as quickly as it appears.

I guess not many tourists want to brave the triple-digit temperatures long enough to hike to the very base of Khafre's Pyramid, but those who do are rewarded with an altogether different experience. There are very few people up here and the cacophony of the tourist scene is replaced by the soft moaning of the warm desert wind. This close, the blocks that compose the pyramid reveal their true mind-boggling size and the pyramid's looming shadow blocks the sun's glare, if not its heat. Up ahead and to the left some local boys are sitting on a boulder talking, and a lone camel rider offers his extra dromedary. I shake my head.

" *La, Shukren.*" (No, thank you, in Egyptian Arabic).

Near the base of the pyramid is a small earthen house, evidently fashioned from the same beige soil it stands on, reminding me of the old Spanish mission of my hometown. To a naive child coming of age in Santa Barbara, the Franciscan mission seemed a romantic architectural epicenter: a stately queen surrounded by historic mudbrick walls and rolling, date-palm shaded lawns. The city's Spanish heritage is cherished by locals and tourists alike, but I wonder how many realize it's as whitewashed as the plaster covering Santa Barbara's ubiquitous red-tile roofed mansions? As I matured, the reality of the Conquistadors' brutality and the Church's intolerance tarnished my enjoyment of the silver-saddled Andalusian horses paraded every year down State Street during the two-week long Old Spanish Days festival, known to Santa Barbara locals as simply: Fiesta.

This small Egyptian mud-brick dwelling, like

the indigenous adobes of Alta California, blends into its environment with an organic grace unmatched by modern architecture. The structure catches my eye because next to the single open door stands a solitary, delicate tree blooming with what looks like bright crimson roses! There is no other vegetation visible as far as the eye can see and I'm reminded of the miracle of the Lady of Guadalupe in 1531 Mexico. When the Aztec mother goddess appeared to humble Juan Diego in the dead of winter, he was given armfuls of rare Castilian red roses—the hallmark of Spanish royalty—to use as proof of his supernatural encounter. The apparition that appeared to the indigenous man halfway around the world from where I'm standing wore a blue cloak covered in golden, five-pointed stars identical to what the Egyptian goddess Isis is often depicted wearing. I did not know it then, but I would see the Virgin of Guadalupe's sacred pattern of golden stars on a blue background many times in the coming days.

Chapter 3

THE PYRAMIDS OF MENKAURE & KHAFRE

After lunch in a Mediterranean restaurant that served couscous in the shape of a pyramid, and whose windows offered a view of the Sphinx, our tour is regrouping again on the Giza plateau for a camel ride to the pyramid of Menkaure. This is the smallest of the Giza pyramids but as rumor has it, also the most magical. We will be among the few visitors who ever actually enter the monument. The pyramid's original height was 215 feet, less than half the size of the Great Pyramid. Like the Great Pyramid, the Pyramid of Menkaure is constructed of limestone and red granite quarried from Aswan, a city 600 miles up the Nile river near ancient Nubia. Even today, no one really knows how these enormous megaliths were transported from Aswan to Giza. Though the Great Pyramid once wore a smooth sheath of white limestone, the Pyramid of Menkaure was finished with a casing of red granite on the lower portion, with the limestone covering the upper portion. Perhaps this explains the pyramids reputation for encharming visitors. The iron, quartz, magnetite, and hematite in Aswan red granite has an electromagnetic effect on human blood and brain tissue, though more research is needed to document exactly what those effects are. Maybe I will know soon.

First we must get there and I'm looking forward to the camel ride almost as much as entering the pyramid. We are gathered on the far side of the tour bus parking area where nothing competes with the view over the famous Giza Plateau. Nothing except an astonishing collection of saddled dromedaries! The knobby-kneed ungulates mill about lazily, their thick, frayed lead ropes falling from aloof heads into the hands of their Egyptian handlers, or more often, draping to the aft horn of another camel's saddle, making a living train of sorts. Each animal wears a nylon halter, similar to a horse halter, through which a metal lead chain is threaded—the kind one might see under the chin of a spirited stallion. I notice the chains appear to be clipped to the halter D-rings and not attached to the large hoop in each animal's nostril.

The towering beasts are tacked up with simple saddle pads under two–horned saddles. One cylindrical horn is positioned in front like a western horse saddle and an additional horn faces backwards on the rear edge of the seat. There are no stirrups of any kind. Exquisitely patterned kilim-style rugs embellished with colorful dangling fringe and braided borders are draped and secured over the saddle trees. Many camels also sport neck coverings with vivid yarn tassels as big as oranges. If that weren't enough, the most flamboyant beasts are further adorned with an additional choker of exotic, brightly dyed pom poms high on their necks.

All the camels, with the exception of a couple of milky beauties, are the color of the sand on which they are now being asked to get down on. This will allow us to mount them for the ride. The crowd is gently surging forward and I find myself at the front of the line, next to Michael, our tour leader. Michael is an expert on temples of all kinds, the best-selling author of books on ancient sites, sacred geometry, and crop circles. Before this morning, I'd only seen him on television shows and YouTube videos. He's much taller than I expected.

A suede-colored beast that looks elegant, if slightly aged, is presented to me. She folds her long front legs underneath her and kneels in what looks like the downward dog yoga pose before dropping her back haunches with a thump on the desert floor. Her Egyptian handler motions me forward.

"Your wife's camel," he says to Michael.

"Oh, I'm not his…"

"Come along Dear," Michael replies, "and get on your camel."

The wrangler's hand reaches out and takes mine, moving me into position to mount the waiting dromedary.

I've ridden horses for years. Add to that the leg strength I've developed as an Egyptian belly dance teacher (the trick to a good shimmy is strong thighs) and I feel well prepared to get on this camel. She is much larger the closer I get, however, and my little leg which used to slide over the back of my chunky ranch gelding barely reaches the other side of this girl's hump.

"Hold on to this," my Egyptian instructor demonstrates, grabbing the front horn of the saddle with his dark, leathered hand. "You must lean back when she stands up. Lean back when she stands up."

"Hang on," Michael advises, taking a skillful seat on the showpiece camel he has been assigned. Without delay his mount reverses the series of moves my girl just demonstrated, rocking forward and then backwards to a standing position.

I nod to my camel wrangler like a professional bull rider ready to leave the chute. He gives the command and my beast's rump rises. And then rises some more. I'm leaning back and gripping the horn with all my strength but this camel's gone vertical! I can sense her rump inches behind my head and I'm really high in the air. I continue to brace as hard as I can against the horn, my thighs tightening in vain atop the wobbling saddle when I feel myself starting to pitch forward. Uh oh! I'm going to fall forward onto this camel's neck!

I've barely grasped the fact that I'm sliding when I realize the lurch forward was caused by her front legs extending up to standing. I'm sitting atop a fully upright camel! The whole debacle, taking mere moments, has been exceedingly worth it. I feel like a queen high above the sands.

From my exalted throne I watch the others in our group being led to their beasts. For the most part everyone mounts successfully, though not all on the first try. I'm relieved to see some of the more mature women in our party safely up.

Settled on our camels, our caravan of modern day mystics sets out across the sand toward the pyramids of Giza. We ride in silence, to the rhythm of dinner plate sized cloven hooves pushing through the sand and saddles gently rocking. Only the wranglers' gentle reprimands in Arabic punctuate the dream. The warm desert wind sings her eternal song. I hear it in my heart and smile.

***

We've ridden for nearly an hour and are finally beside the Pyramid of Menkaure. Though it's the smallest of the three Giza pyramids it is still startlingly huge. Our Egyptian guide Shani is standing on the sand, conferring with several official looking men. Michael is leaning down from his camel, listening. Then he sits up straight.

"Well, change of plans," he announces to the semicircle of camel riders assembled in front of the pyramid.

A neighbor's camel starts to sit down with the rider aboard but the handler smacks it with a thick stick and it straightens back up.

"The Pyramid of Menkaure is closed. It is too humid in there today. It's not safe to go in."

Groans and sighs float above the desert floor. My heart falls, shot with an arrowhead of disappointment tipped with relief. I have been secretly afraid to go down into the pyramids. Well, not totally secret. Sara was with me in Tokyo a few years ago when I suffered a claustrophobic meltdown in a closet-sized Tokyo elevator. And to clarify, it was coat-closet sized, not walk-in closet. The windowless death box led down to an underground robot show. There was no other way to attend the show. I had been successfully coaxed in by my daughter and Sara and the lift was absolutely, completely full when six more Japanese people pushed in and the doors closed. Like sardines, but tighter. Meditate, meditate. I willed myself into silence but felt like screaming. It will only be seconds, I told myself, just breathe. Then the doors slid open but we were not at the venue. We were back where we started! Three Australian guys had summoned the elevator mid-descent and were stepping in! And they were strapping big Aussies.

"No! Please!" I begged, or maybe screamed.

They must have sensed the vibe of a hysterical Sheila, because they immediately backed away.

"No worries, mate," the handsome fella said, "we'll take the next one."

The sound of a button being depressed (I couldn't see the control panel through the sardines) and the elevator doors again slid shut. Probably thirty seconds later they clacked open. We walked to our seats. When the show ended and lights illuminated the audience area, I noticed there was an EXIT sign behind a velvet curtain. I was elated when I located a door. Behind it were cement stairs that delivered me blissfully into the crisp Harajuku night air. Next time, I promised myself, I'll come in through the out door.

"Instead," Michael continued, snapping me back to where I was, on the back of a camel in Egypt, staring at the pyramids of Giza, "This afternoon we will go down into the Pyramid of Khafre."

***

I, a pyramid virgin, am descending the narrow, rock-cut shaft of the Pyramid of Khafre. Khafre's is the middle pyramid of the three on the Giza Plateau, sited in between the Great Pyramid and the Pyramid of Menkaure. We have been diverted to this monument because extreme humidity made our planned excursion into the smaller Pyramid of Menkaure too dangerous. Though we entered from a different side of the structure, this is the same pyramid I walked up to from the Sphinx. I suspect I am about halfway down the 100 foot subterranean stone shaft because I can't see either the brilliant sunlit aperture of entry, nor the basalt passageway to the inner chamber at the bottom. Like most pyramid shafts, this one is not tall enough to stand up in, even for a 5' 4" woman, so I double over and crouch my way down. The width of the tunnel does allow two people to pass one another other if necessary, but sides are brushed in the process. Only solid, immovable stone surrounds me–and people. Above and below me in the sweltering rock tube they climb, breathing the air I need, boxing me in! I had worried that claustrophobia might catch me underground inside the pyramids. Now I feel it close, ready to pounce.

I'd like to run, but a line of people is choking the shaft both upward and down, so instead I press myself against the bedrock wall of the dimly lit tunnel like a rabbit huddling in its burrow. I can feel my clothes clinging to my clammy, cortisol-soaked body. The crushing humidity creates a feeling of being buried alive. Is this what it feels like inside a sarcophagus? I focus on breathing, or rather, not suffocating. Empathetic fellow tunnelers have halted their descent behind me; at this point we have essentially become one long segmented organism, moving in unison like a human centipede. I close my eyes and remember Jean Houston's book *The Passion of Isis and Osiris*. In it, she wrote that the neters can always be called upon to help us so over the deafening drumbeat of my heart, I silently beseech the gods for help.

Within moments, a most unexpected thing happens. A delicate breeze is caressing my face, laminar and fresh. Inexplicably, it seems to be blowing up from the inky depths below. I inhale deeply and a cool, pencil–slim serpent of air slithers into my nostrils, refreshing my lungs with the sweetest oxygen, filling my heart with calmness. This experience isn't a visualization, it's distinct and somatic, as if someone has slipped an invisible cannula of oxygen into my nose.

But something even stranger is happening. Beside me, I perceive two women. I somehow see them, but not with my eyes. They are beautiful and happy, tangible but invisible.

We'll be here with you, they assure me, the message entering my consciousness like birdsong on a summer's day.

The rock no longer seems to contain me. My anxiety has evaporated into an almost giddy state of fearless curiosity. My rational mind is struggling to process what is happening while my spirit body—what the Egyptians called the ka—continues interacting with my ethereal friends.

Who are you? I inquire telepathically.

Isis, the name shivers like ice through my nerves. *And Hathor*, a second electrical storm explodes through my cells, blooming into gooseflesh on my skin.

So I start moving down the shaft formerly known as claustrophobic feeling psychologically liberated, my girls by my side. My fellow explorers seem surprised by my sudden confidence but they don't say a thing; they are relieved our human centipede is on the move again.

I am delighted and bewildered. I can't stop smiling. Yes, I have had some strange experiences before, but I am not prone to spiritual hyperbole. Isis? Really? Even if I have imagined the goddesses—perhaps they were a desperate conjuring by a clever, Egypt-obsessed psyche—what explains the actual physical feeling of air blowing up against my face? What explains the indisputable relief of chilled oxygen flowing down into my grateful lungs? What could possibly explain my utter lack of claustrophobia as I happily crawl down the fifty additional feet of this cramped, crowded, underground rock tunnel?

Back at the hotel that evening I send a text to my family: I went down inside my first pyramid today!

Chapter 4

THE PYRAMID
OF
UNAS

A solitary Egyptian man, so the story goes, was out hunting when he spotted a jackal trotting across the desert. He tracked the animal for some time, for it seemed to be navigating the featureless landscape with keen intention and familiarity, almost tempting the man to follow. After a time, they came upon a pile of rubble and stone, and the man watched as the jackal climbed up and disappeared into a rock! Upon closer inspection, a crack was found in the boulder, which led down into the earth. This rubble, once excavated, turned out to be one of the wonders of Saqqara: the pyramid of King Unas of the Fifth Dynasty, circa 2,345 BCE.

The pharaohs of the Fifth dynasty were apparently unrelated to those of the previous Dynasty. The Fourth Dynasty pharaoh Khufu (Cheops) and his son Khafre (Chephren) are linked by name to the pyramids of Giza. Yet all the Fifth Dynasty Pharaohs—of whom Unas was the last—are said to have been children of a High Priestess of the Sun god Ra, hailing from Heliopolis. Born into the magic of the Old Religion, Unas may have foreseen the beginning of the end of Egypt's glorious Old Kingdom, for he left, beneath the sands of Saqqara, a sacred gift to posterity.

I'm making my way down the descending shaft of the Pyramid of Unas. I've decided to go with the forward facing crouching walk technique, as this solid rock tunnel, like many pyramid shafts, measures only about 4.5 feet, both high and wide. It's a long, steeply–sloped trek down. In the dimly lit passageway, a woman in front of me has turned around on the wooden causeway and is stepping down backwards. My view is the top of her head and her hands gripping the side rails as she steps blindly backwards, her sneakers feeling for the crossbars blessedly placed on the narrow wooden ramp to prevent slipping. I dabbled in the backwards descent and while it does relieve the thigh burn, I found it too slow. Plus, I don't want to look only at wooden boards between my legs for the forty-seven feet it takes to reach the vestibule at the bottom of this subterranean shaft. Not that I have much of a view this way, but when I'm forced to wait for someone to catch their breath—or their courage—I can kneel down and caress the smooth stone walls or place my palm against the alarmingly close ceiling of the shaft, and remind myself happily that I'm inside an Egyptian pyramid!

After navigating the descending shaft and traversing a stone hallway of sorts, one ultimately enters the underground antechamber, a twelve by ten foot limestone vestibule with an elegant pitched roof. Every inch of the walls is covered, top to bottom, with small, delicate, and impeccably carved hieroglyphics! I feel like I've wandered into a futuristic virtual reality room with binary code composing the walls, except instead of ones and zeros streaming, there are 283 magical spells incised in neat, vertical columns on the sandstone walls surrounding me. They are so precisely carved, so perfectly preserved, it's difficult to believe they are over 4,000 years old. Up to the ceiling the chapters rise, revealing spiritual secrets once reserved for High Priestesses, Pharaohs and the most privileged initiates. These are walls of *heka* (magic).

Known as the Pyramid Texts, they are a travel guide for the disembodied soul, an explanation of multidimensional existence, and a primer of incantations that bestow spiritual power to the astral voyager.

The thousands of utterances carved elegantly into the initiation chamber of this monument may be the oldest surviving link between magical predynastic Egypt and the Old Kingdom—the beginning of humanity's modern recorded history. I'm calling it an initiation chamber because the body of Unas was not found interred here, nor was anyone else's. Despite what most of us have been taught in school, no mummies have ever been found in any of the oldest Egyptian Pyramids, including those at Saqqara, Dahshur, and the three most famous in Giza.

What we do know is sometime circa 2,300 BCE, Unas constructed this pyramid, committing to stone what was an ancient oral tradition of practical spiritual knowledge.

Later transcribed to papyrus and tucked beside the deceased during burial rituals, these spells became known as *The Egyptian Book of the Dead*, or as the Egyptians called it, *The Book of Coming Forth by Light*.

Leaning back, looking up at the perfectly pitched, vaulted ceiling, it's hard to believe that four thousand years have passed since an anonymous artist created this celestial canopy, its stone firmament shining with five-pointed stars of gold on a background of Egyptian blue. Remarkably, the original paint color can still be seen in some areas, though the decoration is fading day by day—a result of the humidity created by the bodies of tourists like myself. I feel grateful. And guilty.

I've decided I'm ready to explore further, to follow my compatriots through a very low, crumbling square doorway and into the intimate alcove that holds Unas' black stone sarcophagus. Suddenly, an agitated Egyptian official in a brown *galabeya* bursts into the subterranean chamber. This guard is confronting our American tour leader in heated Arabic, pointing to the exit shaft, compelling our Egyptian guide to intervene. Shani is a kind Egyptian woman well-versed in the history and mythology of ancient Khem, but she is also responsible for our group's well-being. Despite her diminutive five–foot–two size and completely unveiled head, she steps right into the commotion with the confidence of a mother grizzly. An acerbic argument echoes off the ancient stone walls until, finally, the guard storms away. Shani explains that even though we were just admitted, the Pyramid is closing early for the day. Whether this is due to dangerous humidity levels or whim is uncertain, so Shani sets off with a fist–full of Egyptian pounds to assuage the aggressive guard. It doesn't work.

A galabeya is a full length cotton or linen robe traditionally worn by Egyptian men. These long shirt-dresses are still ubiquitous in Egypt today and you'll find men wearing them everywhere—from your hotel valet to local farmers working their fields to official monument guards.

The official appears again, singling me out. His dark eyes narrow and his voice rises as he gestures with his left arm toward the exit route. His English is rough but his intention obvious. His plastic name tag says Mamoud. Standing shoulder to shoulder with Mamoud is Michael, who is an imposing six-foot-five. Michael's pointing to the right–urging me toward the sarcophageal chamber.

"Go in there!" Michael exhorts.

Two formidable men, commanding me forcefully in opposite directions, are engaged in a palpable power struggle two feet in front of me. I'm frozen, my eyes darting from one face to the other. The official is irritated that his authority is being challenged and I've heard stories of what can happen when a western woman flouts middle–eastern rules. But when I look at Michael, I feel a force field of sorts, almost like a protective bubble.

"Go in there now!" he implores again. I may never be here again, fifty feet underground in the 4,000 year old sanctum of King Unas, so I duck under Michael's outstretched arm and dart like a mouse through the small hole that leads into the most sacred chamber of the Pyramid of Unas.

I have never seen a stone sarcophagus before and I'm shocked. Not only at the sight and size of the jet black receptacle, but that some people are actually climbing into it and taking pictures! I don't mind, it's just that the teachings previously shared with us advise a pilgrimage of energetic upgrades before entering a sarcophagus.

The monuments of Egypt are more than beautiful buildings—they are interactive environments designed and created to affect the electromagnetic bodies of humans. From the quartz, iron, and magnetite in the masonry, to the geometric matrixes of the architecture, to the esoteric siting, Egyptian temples can enhance consciousness—or short-circuit those not adequately prepared. In ancient times, initiates traveled the Nile, stopping at each magnificent riverside temple, paying homage to the Neter–in–Residence while receiving the energetic blessing of the monument itself. Subtle enhancements—both spiritual and physical—resulted in a human gently transformed and better equipped to benefit from the potent energies concentrated inside a sarcophagus contained within a pyramid.

Fearing we'll be out-adventured, my competitive streak dismisses such wisdom and spurs me on into the sarcophagus. But my heart stops us. Not yet. Michael believes this chamber was never meant to house a corpse, but was created for sacred ritual, designed to facilitate shamanic visions or actual astral travel to the *Dwat,* "the Egyptian otherworld, a place as real to the Egyptians as the physical world. However, unlike the physical world…this parallel place exists outside of time; it is present and eternal, and simultaneous with the physical."[1]

I place my palms on top of the polished walls of the open box. They are thick, maybe eight inches wide, and it's deeper than expected. On the nearest wall is a portion of the Pyramid Texts carved in 2,350 BCE. These hieroglyphics are known as Utterance 213, and proclaim:

> *O King Unas!*
> *You have not gone away dead!*
> *You have gone away alive!*
>
> *You sit upon the throne of Osiris.*
> *Your power-scepter in your hand,*
> *that you may give orders to the living.*
> *Your lotus-bud scepter in your hand,*
> *that you may give orders to the dead.*

I imagine Unas rising from this box, not from the dead, but returning from an out–of–body experience in the underworld, having received a glimpse into another dimension, or as the Egyptians called it "pulling back the veils of Isis."

Quantum physicists now agree that there are at least eleven dimensions of existence, each separated by a mere whisper of vibrational difference. Is it possible the Egyptians possessed a technology to recalibrate their consciousness? To

---

[1] Silva, Freddy. 2014. *The Lost Art of Resurrection Initiation, Secret Chambers, and the Quest for the Otherworld.* Inner Traditions, Rochester, VT, p. 1.

tune their own resonance to another reality and interact with denizens of other frequencies? Was I standing inside that technology?

Exiting the pyramid with the last few stragglers requires filing past the usurped guard who is still lingering in the ante-chamber, stationed at the access point to the exit shaft. I avoid eye contact but feel his scowl on my back as I pass by. Clipping my hair back, I put my head down and begin the lengthy climb up towards ground level. It doesn't take long before I can see the small sunlit hatchway at the top of the shaft becoming ever larger. Minutes later, I emerge like a wily jackal onto the rocky sands of Saqqara.

Chapter 5

THE SERAPEUM

Unas' pyramid is a sacred link to the magic of Egypt's Old Kingdom, but there is something even more mysterious underground beneath the Saqqara complex. A place hardly anyone even knows about. It's not a temple, or a pyramid, and whomever—or whatever—it once held had already vanished without a trace by the time it was first discovered in 1850. We board the bus for a short jaunt to another nearby parking area to discover for ourselves the enigma the Greeks called the Serapeum.

It's a long, gritty walk from the car park through one of the most desolate landscapes on earth. I'm approaching the

Serapeum and I don't think I've ever been as utterly exposed to the elements, surrounded for miles by oven-hot air and flat sand seas. Every so often swells of desert wind splash waves of fine Egyptian sand against my face. The sloshing of the small water bottle in my backpack has taken on sacred significance. Up ahead, a woman drenches a handkerchief with her precious water and ties it around her neck. Across the horizon, light diffracts into sinuous, translucent heat waves, liquifying the distinction between earth and sky. We walk on.

From I don't know where, a local man on a donkey trots up alongside our group. He's riding barefoot, wearing a loose tunic and dark pants. His white scarf is wrapped Bedouin-style around his head. In one hand he holds a Saidi-style stick with which he casually smacks the donkey, positioning himself for his pitch. With unrelenting persistence, he calls out as we pass, motioning to the donkey. He is here to offer rides to anyone discouraged by the trek. I shake my head no but it doesn't take long before a sweaty American is pressing a bank note with the Sphinx on it into his palm.

Our friend who took the four-legged taxi has already dismounted when the rest of our group arrives at the Serapeum. The entrance, it turns out, is an unassuming arched wooden door at the end of a descending, paver-like pathway. Compared to the archaeological glamour of its neighbors—the Step Pyramid, the Bent Pyramid, and the Red Pyramid—one's first impression of the Serapeum might be its lack of curb appeal.

The ancient, weathered sentry who tears the edge off

my sweat-crinkled entry ticket and hands it back appears indifferent, but his wet eyes sparkle when I greet him with the traditional Muslim salutation.

"*Salam Alaikum.*"

"*Walaikum Salam!*" he calls back as I step through the transom.

Salam Alaikum (Peace be upon you) is the Egyptian Arabic pronunciation of a common Muslim greeting. An appropriate reply is Walaikum Salam (And upon you be peace).

The transition from the midday North African sunshine into the cavern-like labyrinth of the Serapeum is like putting on sunglasses. As my eyes adjust, I can see long, rough-hewn underground avenues conveniently fitted with wide wooden boardwalks stretching off in several directions. We descend silently, following the guide, taking it all in. The ambiance is slightly wine-cavey, except that it's soundless, deathlike, and fragranced with the inimitable must of crumbling stone and stories untold. Every so often, improbable blonde masonry arches punctuate the craggy rock tubes, whether for structural support or aesthetic appeal I'm not sure (I'm really hoping the former). Along the sides of the underground avenue, enormous caves have been gouged out. The caverns are crude, unfinished, and the exact opposite of their contents. Tucked inside each of these

TOMB OF THE APIS.

grand niches, nestled four to six feet below the level of the walkways, sits a massive granite box. And by massive I mean seventy tons, with separate lids that themselves weigh thirty tons each.

They're unbelievably, puzzlingly huge, each fashioned from a single piece of black granite, rose granite, or diorite (which is even harder than granite). The most striking thing about these so-called sarcophagi, besides their gargantuan size, are the precision-crafted edges. They feature sharp 90 degree angles, both inside and out, that defy explanation, and would be difficult to recreate today. Many are polished to an impeccable, glossy luster. The accompanying sixty-thousand pound lids match the containers so perfectly as to appear machined. Reportedly "the granite boxes are made with high precision and have a tolerance within 1 micron. So, closing the lid essentially makes them hermetically sealed."[2] In other words, these 100 ton stone storage cubes could withstand anything we can imagine, including a nuclear war or a worldwide flood.

When they were re-discovered in the 1850s by French Egyptologist Auguste Mariette, all but one of the megalithic boxes were found with their lids ajar and nothing inside. Assuming they had been robbed of their treasures, Mariette blasted a hole in the closed box, finding it too, was empty. Perhaps the heady delirium of treasure fever conjured up the ludicrous assumption that tomb robbers could have slid thirty ton stone lids off to remove the contents. But something or someone did.

---

[2]Kborissov. 2022. *Lighting Up Saqqara: An Electrifying Theory for the Serapeum Sarcophagi* (https://www.ancient-origins.net/unexplained-phenomena/serapeum-sarcophagi-021992). Accessed on August 19, 2022.

Almost all of the boxes are still right where they were discovered by Mariette, mainly because there is no feasible way of moving them, even using the best modern minds and technology. The few empty grottoes and one box left in the middle of a tunnel bely past attempts to unsuccessfully move the megalithic artifacts, most of which ended up blasted to bits. There is no evidence they were carved in situ; somehow they were transported here and placed underground. A few of the polished black boxes are embellished with simple Egyptian hieroglyphs and geometric designs that evoke ancient Grecian art, but the comparatively poor quality of the writing has cast speculation on the glyphs antiquity. There is speculation that the glyphs were added in historical times, but there is simply no way of knowing when these decorations were inscribed.

The Serapeum is named for the God Serapis—a combination of Osiris and Apis, the sacred Bull, who was worshipped primarily by the Ptolemaic Greeks of Alexandria (c. 305-30 BCE). Apis bulls were selected at a young age by Egyptian priests specially trained to recognize their godly characteristics, and they were considered to be a vehicle for the soul of Osiris himself. According to the first century CE Greek writer Plutarch: "Apis ought ever to be regarded by us as a fair and beautiful image of the soul of Osiris".[3] When the bulls died they were mourned, mummified, and then buried with the same glory that occurred with the death of a pharaoh.

Though conventional Egyptology accepts the Serapeum as a catacomb for Apis bulls, the hypothesis is

---

[3]Hall, Manley P. 1988. *The Secret Teachings of All Ages.* The Philosophical Research Society Inc, Los Angeles, CA. p. XCI (91)

not as air tight as the boxes themselves. Firstly, the coffers are far too spacious for even the largest Apis bull. The fact that Pharaohs were buried in sarcophagi well sized to their bodies makes it unlikely that mummified bulls were interred in such wastefully large containers, especially considering the challenge of crafting the granite boxes increases with their size. More to the point, no evidence of any mummies or remains (human or bovine) has ever been found associated with the massive stone boxes.

But mummies were found close by.

Adjacent to and at an approximate ninety–degree angle to the Main Gallery (where the gigantic granite coffers are located) there are "Lesser Halls" in the Serapeum where mummified bulls (and one unlucky human fellow) were found entombed in wooden coffins.

Mariette, the Egyptologist who discovered the Serapeum, alluded to the possibility that the mummified bulls were interred in historical times, long after the Serapeum was originally created. In his journals, Mariette wrote: "the new tunnels which we have called "the Little Tunnels," the name of Large Tunnels leaving to the ancient ones, do not have the regularity, the greatness, and the conservation of the others."

Like so many truly ancient and possibly pre-Diluvial sites, the Serapeum includes extraordinary megalithic masonry as well as an obviously less ancient element. The common practice of constructing temples, churches and sacred tombs on sites venerated since antiquity not only confuses the lay historian, but often blatantly contradicts Darwinian evolution. The deeper, older monuments are often made of multi-ton stones, sourced from far afield, and fitted together with such skill that, even today, a piece of paper or credit card cannot be inserted between the blocks. Subsequent strata of use feature stones of declining size and clearly inferior construction techniques.

Our planet's oldest known monuments, Gobekli Tepe in Turkey, the Great Pyramid at Giza, and Stonehenge in Britain, to name just a few, feature complex astronomical alignments and are encoded with nearly unfathomable mathematical magic. The measurements of the Great Pyramid, for example, are related mathematically to the circumference of the Earth, the Great Year of the zodiac (Precession of the Equinoxes), and the orbit of Sirius, as well as being sited with spectacular precision to the four cardinal points: North, South, East, and West. As modern researchers continue to decipher the sophisticated invisible geometry and geomancy of pre-flood megalithic cities—temples and stone circles that are 5,000, 8,000 or even tens of thousands of years old—it's becoming evident that civilization as we know it is not the glittering apex of 5,000 years of Darwinian evolution.

Moreover, the relatively recent, documented uses of a site are often presented as evidence of its original purpose, regardless of sketchy archaeological facts. So the awe-inspiring stone boxes of the Serapeum are written off as sarcophagi for Apis bulls, despite no bovine remains ever having been found inside any of them. The containers' implausibly massive size, precise ninety-degree masonry angles, hermetically designed stone–lid closures, and inexplicable fine, gloss finish are neither emphasized, nor accounted for.

What is mentioned by the very earliest Arabian historians, such as Ibn Abd Alhokm, is that before the great flood the high priests of ancient Egypt created an impenetrable repository for all of their knowledge. Hidden in the Pyramids of Giza or in some other as yet undisclosed location are archives and books containing advanced teachings on astronomy, physics, geometry, healing, spirituality and magic, along with such things like glass that would bend but not break, metal that would not rust, and other intriguing ancient technologies and treasures.

The Giza Pyramids are the obvious possibility, but clearly something was stored in these boxes as well. Additional sacred texts perhaps? Or maybe something even more shocking. It is easy to see why conventional Egyptologists labeled these granite containers sarcophagi. When one sees a purposefully shaped stone box with a lid angled out at one end, the first thought is: coffin. Remember though, no trace of human (or other) remains were found in any of the rock receptacles. Is it possible that whoever was inside these stone boxes arose at some point and stepped out? This is just speculation, but these ancient black boxes seem sized for very tall people, as do so many Egyptian monuments.

Precision-crafted and positioned in their subterranean cellar, the granite boxes of the Serapeum are clearly designed as a repository for something or someone, but what or whom? Did whoever created them come and collect their things after flood waters retreated, pushing aside the 30-ton lids like Tupperware?

The original creators of the Serapeum possessed abilities of masonry and logistics that stretch the limits of what is possible—and practical—in our world. Yet these incredible artifacts exist, right now, on our planet. Were they built by the neters of Egypt? The Followers of Horus? The

Anunnaki? Or a race of beings lost to human memory? To stand before one of these "out of place" artifacts, deep under the sands of Egypt, is to confront the hidden history of our planet head on. Most amazingly, unlike touring a museum, visitors to the Serapeum (at time of writing) can slide a warm hand along the still polished granite and intuit their own insights. No peer-reviewed scientific study or archaeological explanation is necessary, an expedition to the Serapeum is an experience of visceral disclosure.

Chapter 6

THE STEP PYRAMID
OF
DJOSER

The sprawling necropolis and pyramid field that comprises Saqqara is not yet fully excavated, but its most recognizable monument is unlikely to change: the stepped pyramid of Djoser. The Step Pyramid is thought to be the first ever monument made entirely of stone in Egypt. To serious students of Egyptian wisdom, the pyramid's architect is just as legendary. Four hundred years after King Menas came to power as (according to the kings list) the first Pharaoh of "a totally human bloodline,"[4] a remarkable human man became a god. Imhotep was a common man with uncommon vision, who rose through the ranks of Egyptian wisdom to become the most revered temple architect in Egyptian history. A high-priest of Ptah, Imhotep was also a scribe, a vizier, and a gifted healer.

Imhotep built the stepped pyramid for Pharaoh Djoser circa 2,600 BCE, almost five thousand years ago. One accesses the monument through the associated temple, known as Saqqara temple, which is linked to the pyramid by an expansive, walled courtyard. The temple's vast courtyard, magical entry colonnade, and sophisticated sacred geometry was designed and constructed to be nothing less than a physical embodiment of quantum creation. The pyramid's dimensions are said to be the holy numbers of the neters, and its 36–degree triangles later informed the work of Pythagoras. Pythagoras studied in Egypt for twenty-two years as a young man so it is probably no coincidence that his five-pointed stars derived from 90–degree triangles were painted on the ceiling of Unas' sacred subterranean chamber and sewn into the gowns of Isis.

After being underground for the last several excursions, it's refreshing to approach the Mansion of the Gods, the stepped pyramid of Djoser, under a soft robin's egg blue sky. After the chill of the air-conditioned bus, the mid-morning heat is a delicious shock, like a summer pool deck on a wet belly. Fronds of wind fan me like invisible servants as we walk toward the temple's thirty-seven foot Tura limestone pylon. A pylon is a tall wall—a wide tower

---

[4]de Lubicz, R.A. Schwaller. 1982. *Sacred Science: he King of Pharaonic Theocracy.* Inner Traditions, VT, p. 111.

or facade—often found at the entrance to Egyptian temples. Some monuments, like Karnak, have more than one pylon.

The wall of Saqqara temple has 14 doors, but only one is meant for flesh and blood humans. The rest are false doors, perhaps designed to confound unwanted visitors, but more likely meant for *Ka* bodies—the spiritual light bodies the Egyptians believed everyone possessed.

Egyptian science and religion recognized a number of "bodies." The mortal flesh and blood body we walk around in is the *khat*. But we have another body, a quantum-esque energy body called the Ka. The Ka permeates and contains—but is not restricted to—the khat. It is personal and individual, but non-local.

"Unlike the khat, (dense physical body), the Ka body can seemingly walk through walls, float in air and cover vast distances in a moment. In yogic literature there are many reliable accounts of saints and mystics bi-locating (being in two places at once). One explanation for this phenomenon has to do with the Ka body. When the Ka is sufficiently charged it can have a kind of density that can be seen by others. Because the Ka is an etheric double of the person, it looks exactly like him or her."[5]

One's Ka, if suitably energized by proper attitude, spiritual practice, and more esoteric means like sexual alchemy, could survive and travel after death—and sometimes even while the khat (the physical body) was still

---

[5]Kenyon, Tom & Sion, Judi. 2002. *The Magdalen Manuscript The Alchemies of Horus and The Sex Magic of Isis.* ORB Communications, WA, p.p. 115-116.

alive. Energizing and activating one's Ka was an essential part of the process of becoming immortal, which the ancient Egyptians believed was absolutely possible. Sexuality in Egypt was sacred, not only for creating life, but because it was used by the Sem Priests and Priestesses and their devoted initiates for strengthening the Ka.

Fantasy? Or future science? Remember, when Pharaoh Djoser's temple was in use, the stories of the predynastic Egyptian gods or neters had not yet been demoted from history to myth. Jeshua bin Joseph, now known as Jesus Christ, would not be born for another 2,500 years. The Catholic Church's smear campaign against the human body—and female sexuality in particular—was still thousands of years away and unimaginable for a culture whose primary deity, Osiris, was a god of fertility and whose word for life force, Sekhem, literally means "to make erect." Hathor, the most ancient and beloved sky goddess of Egypt was revered as the tutelary goddess of sexuality, dancing, and drunkenness!

I'm daydreaming about the ancient ways, imagining this conscious blending of sensuality and sorcery. Impeccable integrity must be required to wield this sacred form of white magic, which is no doubt why the specific techniques were closely guarded. How easily one could knowingly or unknowingly burn up years of spiritual progress in the flames of desire, or entice another to do the same. But there seems to be a safeguard against this: at a certain level of awareness, many initiates discover it is almost physically impossible to be with a lover broadcasting an incompatible energy signature. The true Magi would rather be alone gathering power than dilute his or her Ka in a relationship of convenience, lust, or security.

We have arrived at the entry to the Saqqara temple. After walking through the door for the living I can see, at the end of a narrow walkway, the sacred Hall of Reeds. The reeds themselves are massive limestone columns crafted to look like bound plant stalks. There are nine "reeds" on each side of the pathway. Their colors are warm and varied like travertine tiles.

"This passageway is unique in that it is a colonnade of 18 reeds separated by narrow alcoves," explains Michael. "Each of the alcoves discharges an alternating field of positive and negatively charged force which serves both as a barrier into the temple while at the same time influencing the body's electromagnetic circuitry. In essence, as one walks down this preparatory hallway into Saqqara, one is suitably entrance-d prior to making contact with the courtyard temple and the mansion of the gods. In its time, this was the procedure necessary for dispelling negative thoughts and emotions one may be harboring before entering the sacred abode."

We are invited to step through the passage individually and slowly walk the hallway, through the Hall of Reeds, trying to sense the energies, seeing what comes up.

Strolling through the colonnade, I sense inhalations and exhalations. My breath pulls powerfully inward then releases slowly outward in effortless synchronicity with the architecture. Energy ebbs and flows like a strong tide, pulling my attention with it. It feels like the temple is breathing. Is this what they mean when they talk about living temples? Are my feet still on the ground?

Emerging through the final two reeds, I walk out of the pathway, feeling a little loopy.

"Did you feel anything?" asks Michael.

"No, but I think I heard the temple breathing," I respond, before stumbling my way toward the site's vast courtyard.

We walk a portion of the courtyard's perimeter as a group, the rectangular inner space stretching away from us like a wide California beach. The courtyard is 613 feet long by 354 feet wide—or roughly the size of two American football fields. At the far (short) end of the rectangle stands the pyramid, soaring over 200 feet into the Egyptian sky. This very place is where Pharaoh Djoser's Heb Sed festival was held in his thirtieth year of reign. The multi-day ritual was meant to show off the Pharaoh's virility and strength, and document his continued god-given right to rule. Should all go well on his thirtieth, he could look forward to repeating the spectacle every few years of his rule thereafter.

Amongst pageantry, feasting, and ceremony, the public portion of the Heb Sed required the pharaoh to run naked around the courtyard, or in some accounts, to chase down a sacred bull and tug on its tail. Encyclopedia Britannica claims a hybrid story—that the king, wearing a short kilt-like garment with a tail affixed to the rear, would run four times around the track.[6] Suffice to say some feat of physical prowess was performed in front of the pleased crowd.

There was another, more mysterious aspect of the Heb Sed. This was a private matter between the Pharaoh and

---

[6]The Editors of Encyclopedia Britannica. *Heb-Sed Egyptian feast (https://www.britannica.com/topic/Heb-Sed)*. Accessed on August 19, 2022.

Sem Priest (High Priest). During this ceremony the pharaoh "dies" and is no longer seen on earth. When he reappears in glorious raiment he bears a sacred papyrus scroll that contains the testament of his father in the neterworld, Osiris.[7]

Osiris is the benevolent, sacrificial god of Egypt who, after being murdered by his brother Set, is ensnared in a tamarisk tree, only to be found and resurrected by his wife Isis. Using magical spells (heka) Isis manages to vivify Osiris long enough to conceive a child: Horus. But then he is murdered a second time by Set, and dismembered. When Isis is unable to re-member Osiris, he becomes Lord of the Underworld, where he shepherds the newly deceased and sanctifies the reigning pharaoh. "Osiris expressed the Christ consciousness of his day…and was an earlier template for the life, death, and resurrection of Jesus." [8]

For the pharaoh, the symbolic Heb Sed resurrection may indeed have been a spiritual journey to the neterworld, albeit assisted by specially prepared plant medicines such as the hallucinogenic blue water lily, or even dangerous poisons expertly administered to trigger near death experiences.

[The ritual] "was conducted hidden from view and involved the administering of secret rites to ensure the Pharaoh's rebirth. He entered a special room carrying the standard of Wepawet—the jackal-headed god whose title Opener of the Ways, is highly suggestive of his function…He was joined by a sem priest who conducted funerary rites… All this preparation for the Pharaoh's embarkation into the

---

[7]Houston, Jean. 1995. *The Passion of Isis and Osiris.* Ballantine/Wellspring (Random House), NY, p. 168.

[8]McCannon, Tricia. 2015. *The Return of the Divine Sophia.* Bear & Company, VT, p. 459.

Photo by Dmitrii Zhodzishkii, courtesy of Unsplash

afterlife is very odd considering he is in perfect health and at the height of his power." [9]

When the Pharaoh reappeared wearing a white garment, he was considered spiritually renewed, his reign consecrated by the gods themselves.

I'm trying to imagine the Heb Sed Festival, but all I can see is pale dirt. We've been released to wander and I'm climbing around some ruins closer to the pyramid when I find myself atop a portion of the crumbling temple wall. I can see others from my group exploring like miniature ant people down at the other end of the courtyard. It seems I am alone with the Step Pyramid. All around me, large boulders sit in silence and I select one as a meditation spot. Settling cross-legged on the rock, I close my eyes and breathe. The doting breeze who once fanned me like royalty has gone, leaving my linen pants wrinkled and my ponytail stuck to my neck with perspiration. Inhale. Hold. Exhale.

I hear activity behind me. Words in Arabic. Getting closer. Sounds like two people. Male voices. I keep my eyes closed like a child, thinking I'll make myself invisible by not looking. I'm not frightened, I just don't want to deal with the panhandling I know is coming. The crunching of gravel comes very close to my left side and I reluctantly open my eyes to an Egyptian man. He's wearing a stained grey galabeya and a snow white scarf wrapped improbably atop a navy baseball cap. He has kind eyes and a wide smile of huge white teeth that don't quite touch each other. His strong

---

[9]Silva, Freddy. 2014. *The Lost Art of Resurrection Initiation, Secret Chambers, and the Quest for the Otherworld.* Inner Traditions, Rochester, VT, p.p. 197, 198.

jawline is sporting a day's stubble. He takes a step towards my rock but I cut him off.

"I'm praying" I explain, putting my hands together in front of my chest.

"Oh," he understands immediately and respectfully backs away.

That worked better than I thought it would. I close my eyes, willing them away, but soon I hear the second man approaching. I squint an eye open and peer out from under my hat to take a look at the sidekick. He's wearing a light brown striped galabeya and a tasseled keffiyeh scarf tied rakishly around his neck. His head is also wrapped with a white fabric. And he's walking closer.

That's when man number one grabs him back. A stern scolding whispered in Egyptian Arabic lets me know my adorable new friend has defended my sacred practice, which I am now feeling slightly guilty about. I *was* trying to meditate, but praying? I'm a recovering Catholic and the word can still make me cringe. My eyes are still closed but I hear them scratching around behind me. It's getting to be a bit much. I decide to return to the group and clamber off the boulder, walk-skipping toward the large courtyard and whoa! I am a lot higher up on this ancient wall than I realized. It's a good six or seven feet straight down to the courtyard level.

The fellas see my predicament and respond in a flash. I consider my options. The hike back the way I came will be circuitous and tediously long in this scorching, breezeless heat. I wonder if anyone has even noticed I'm gone?

My man and his friend are already down the wall in the courtyard gravel, holding their arms up as if coaxing a cat out of a tree. In a moment of absolute trust, I hand my backpack down to the wing man and from a squatting position, let myself fall ever so slightly forward until my hands are on my new friend's wide shoulders. As I do, two strong hands close around my ribcage and I am floated in a gentle arc to the temple soil.

He releases me the moment my feet touch the ground and we both smile and laugh. Wing Man hands me my pack. Wing Man knows a few English phrases but the other man clearly does not. We're all trying to learn each other's names. I hear my friend say Callan once, but I never do grasp his name. Extracting my phone from my backpack, I motion to Wing Man to please take our picture. This he understands. My friend and I are having a great time, giggling at nothing in particular. Posing for the photo, he places a gentlemanly hand lightly on my shoulder leaving a generous buffer of air between our bodies. I soon discover the other guy is a joker and a player, obviously well-practiced at charming *backsheesh* (tips) out of tourists and he soon goes to work on me. I wonder if this is their livelihood, asking for backsheesh from temple visitors. Where might they live? We seem far from any town or village. I look closely at the dark faces, trying to figure out how old they are. Twenties? Thirties? Forties? They seem youngish, but I really have no idea.

I'm trying to tell Wing Man that I'm not rich which of course sounds ridiculous considering I'm an American woman who has flown to Egypt for a vacation. There's no way to explain that I've sold my publishing business (into which I put my life savings and then some) and I'm using the last of the modest profits to fulfill a lifelong dream, retirement fund

be damned! The truth is I would love to give them money. A lot of money. All the cash in my bag. But something is stopping me. I don't want our relationship to be that.

"No backsheesh," I explain, putting my hand over my heart. "We're friends."

"Friends," my man smiles at me and then repeats it to the other fella in a decidedly not-friendly tone.

Wing Man knows his gig is up and cracks his own endearing grin. The good nature coming off these guys is palpable. They have no idea how exotic they look to me. I didn't know men like this actually existed. An absurd and fleeting fantasy of bringing them back to America flashes through my mind, and I realize it is their joy I want to take home with me. This is a souvenir they give freely. They escort me back, one man on each side like bodyguards as we walk across the vast, sun-caked courtyard where Pharaoh Djoser performed in his Heb Sed Festival 4,600 years ago. Once in sight of my tour group, the Egyptian men break away like fighter jets and are gone.

I walk the rest of the way back to the soundtrack of my sneakers on gravel. My mind returns to the man who built this complex. Who, really, was this Imhotep guy?

Imhotep was a priest-physician-architect who lived at the dawn of Egypt's Golden Age, circa 2690-2613 BCE Imhotep authored the now famous Edwin-Smith Papyrus, which describes successful surgical procedures performed 4,500 years ago!

Egyptian medicine employed a multifaceted

treatment program. Sound healing techniques included frequencies generated by sacred tools as well as toning and incantation of magic words or heka by the physician-magi. Only high priests and priestesses knew the proper intonation of the heka, whose power could be used to vex as well as heal. This is likely the origin of the idea of putting a hex on someone by way of speaking a magical spell.

Sound wasn't the only Egyptian medicine. Herbs, tonics, and unguents sourced from environments near and far were utilized to heal various ailments and for practical purposes like pregnancy tests. Ancient Egyptian women soaked bags of wheat or barley with their urine. The resulting effect on the grains' growth would not only determine pregnancy, but also the sex of the unborn child. In 1973, the researcher Colin Ronan reported that under scientific investigation, the "spell" actually did predict pregnancy although it would be thousands of years before western society rediscovered a similar method of detecting pregnancy.[10]

Ronan also noted that a four thousand-year old tomb painting in Beni Hassan shows contraceptives being made from acacia spikes, honey, and dates. Four millennia later, scientists came to realize that acacia spikes contain lactic acid, a known spermicide. It makes one wonder about the ancient spell "How to Turn an Old Man into a Youth", which used a pulp ground from the (regrettably unidentified) hemayet plant to remove wrinkles and age spots.[11]

---

[10]Houston, Jean. 1995. *The Passion of Isis and Osiris.* Ballantine/ Wellspring (Random House), NY, p. 171. (sourced from *Lost Discoveries* by Colin Ronan, MacDonald, NY, 1973, p.p. 83-84)

[11]Ibid.

The Egyptians reputation as "the healthiest race of the ancient world,"[12] was not simply a result of sophisticated wild-crafting, vibrational recalibration, and skilled surgeons. Treatments and medicines were applied on specific days and months, whose astronomical alignments would facilitate effectiveness. Revolutionary Egyptologist John Anthony West elucidates, "It is clear that Egyptian medicine had a strong astrological element. The papyri advise specific times at which to administer specific recipes. Modern medicine knows nothing of such things, but accumulating evidence begins to reveal the existence of cycles and periodicities in the incidence of diseases and their intensities...Anthroposophical experiments have shown that mineral salt solutions are sensitive to planetary influences (as is the sap of plants), while the work of Italian chemist Georgio Piccardi has shown that colloidal suspensions are sensitive to influences that seem to be extra-galactic."[13]

In ancient Egypt, spiritual, mental, and emotional wounds were as important to treat as physical trauma. People suffering from such maladies were welcome to sleep in the sacred vibration of the temple to receive healing dreams, insights, and cures, watched over by priestesses trained in the healing arts. Perhaps, someday, this holistic approach will be embraced again, and health won't be defined simply as the absence of disease, but the presence of joy, wisdom and spiritual fulfillment.

---

[12]West, John Anthony. 1995. *Serpent in the Sky The High Wisdom of Ancient Egypt.* Quest Books Theosophical Publishing House, IL, p.p. 125-126

[13]West, John Anthony. 1995. *Serpent in the Sky The High Wisdom of Ancient Egypt.* Quest Books Theosophical Publishing House, IL, p. 119

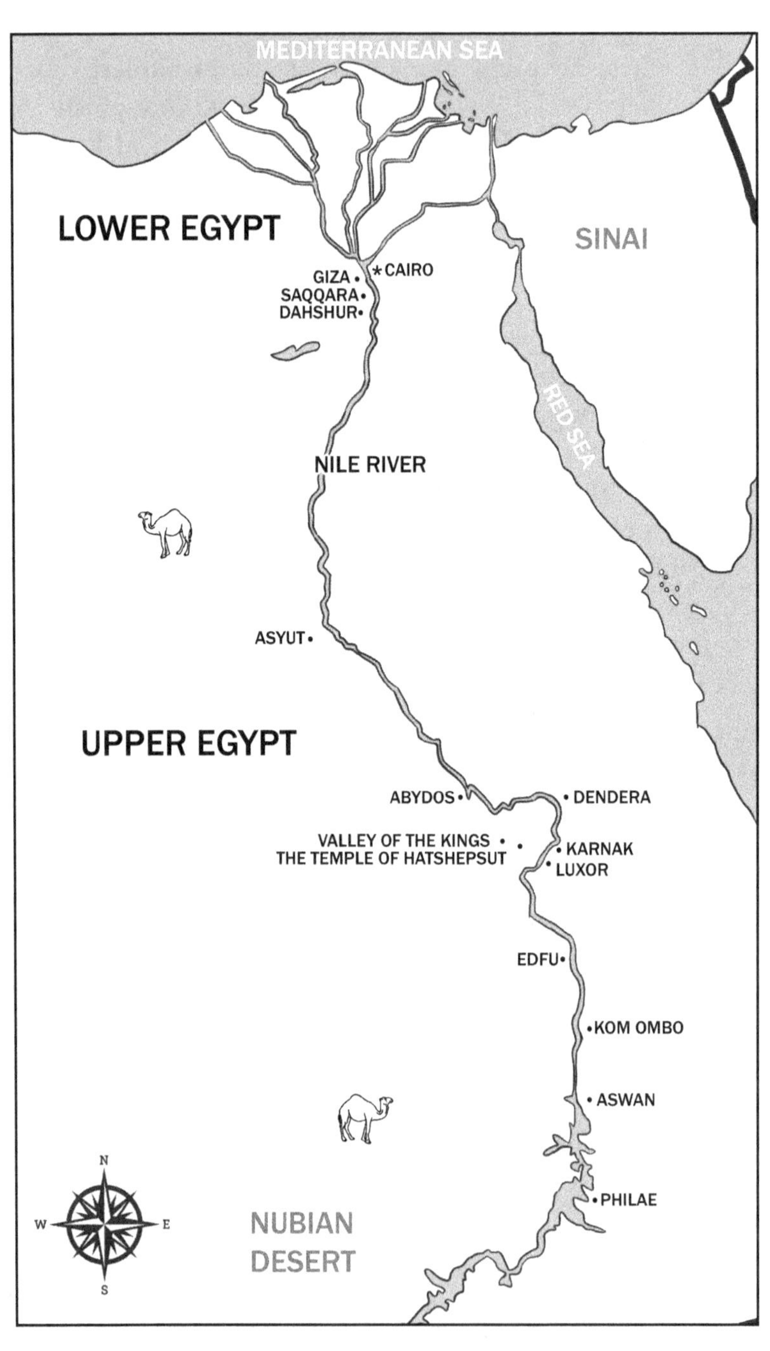

MEDITERRANEAN SEA
LOWER EGYPT
SINAI
GIZA
SAQQARA
DAHSHUR
CAIRO
RED SEA
NILE RIVER
ASYUT
UPPER EGYPT
ABYDOS
DENDERA
VALLEY OF THE KINGS
THE TEMPLE OF HATSHEPSUT
KARNAK
LUXOR
EDFU
KOM OMBO
ASWAN
PHILAE
N
W
E
S
NUBIAN
DESERT

Chapter 7

THE
BENT PYRAMID

Long ago I was approaching a remote South Pacific island from a sailboat at sea. Far off, on the vast and watery horizon, a tiny triangular mound appeared to float. It grew as we got closer and I could see it wore a narrow emerald green ring at the bottom edge where it touched the sea. After passing over a coral reef, its former pyramidal shape morphed into craggy lush mountains. When we sailed into a wide bay I realized the string-thin green line was actually a fringe of towering palm trees bordering the island's beaches. Above the swaying trees, the majestic mountains seemed to climb into the heavens themselves. Our once mighty ship bobbed offshore, as delicate and inconsequential as a white Plumeria petal floating on the waves.

Substitute endless rocky sand for the sea, a forty-nine foot casing of ancient ivory-colored limestone for the palm trees and a gleaming white tourist coach for the catamaran and you'd be approaching Egypt's iconic Bent Pyramid of Dahshur. This structure is 344 mind-blowing feet tall. Unlike any other Egyptian pyramid, the sides are built using two distinct angles. About two thirds of the way up, the slope changes from 54 degrees, "bending" to a shallower 43 degree construction. Closed since 1965, it was reopened to tourists only two months ago. I am one of a handful of lucky visitors climbing the stomach-tickling wooden staircase that hugs the exterior western wall of the pyramid. Built to facilitate tourism, the dizzying platform offers access to the slope-side western entrance of this mysterious monument.

We're waiting for an official to unlock the wooden double doors that protect the sacred entry portal from god knows who. Besides our group clustered under the slatted wooden roof of the narrow entry platform, there are only a handful of tourists sprinkled like pepper grains on the sand below. Farther out on the barren grounds, a solitary Egyptian guard in a billowing white short-sleeved shirt and dark beret is circumnavigating the pyramid on an ATV. Beyond him, only white sand. For miles. It feels like we're flying above the earth, but when I turn around, massive 4,600 year old casing stones angle skyward, close enough to touch. Twenty-five modern pilgrims huddle on the wooden scaffolding. Our bubbles of personal space have long since intertwined, creating a colorful tapestry of energetic vesica Pisces floating like a magic carpet high above the Egyptian desert.

The shaded benches, in addition to being terrifyingly positioned on the outside edge of the entry structure, are rightly taken by the oldest, sweatiest, and shortest of breath. I step out onto the sunny, westward facing ledge to pose for an impromptu portrait with the pyramid.

This is when they unlock the doors. We all file into the stone hole as if it's the most natural thing. It is not.

The descending shaft of the Bent Pyramid, like most Old Kingdom pyramids, is solid stone, rectangular, about four feet wide, and not tall enough to stand up in—even for a five-foot-four woman. And it's a long one; 256 feet of dimly lit limestone slopes down from the pyramid's western ingress to the lowermost antechamber, which is below ground level. Leaning forward, I grasp the wooden handrails. They look as if they fall away into the inner earth. With eager anticipation, I lower my head and climb downward.

There are two chambers hidden deep in the heart of the Bent Pyramid. The first one we encounter is the subterranean cavity. Apparently there's a hole at the top through which the secondary chamber can be located. Having completed the long descent, I pass through a stone doorway and can finally stand up straight, stretching my back and legs. It's actually not uncomfortably hot in here, deep under the earth, insulated from the baking Dahshur desert inside 43,685,655 cubic feet of limestone. What I'm not expecting is the spectacular corbelled ceiling of the antechamber. It's so tall and so narrow, it feels more like a large vertical shaft than a chamber. Rising upward, the stacked limestone slabs encroach ever inward, squeezing the space slimmer and slimmer the higher one goes. And one does go, because in front of me, nearly filling the subterranean sanctum, is a roughly built open-sided wooden staircase, winding back on itself like stiff, squared-off DNA. It's so tall that I can't see the top from where I'm standing, even with the helpful light of the naked incandescent bulbs clinging to the studs. I can see a vast series of two-by-fours wedged tightly between the stair structure and the adjacent stone walls. My first thought is National Treasure. The movie, I mean. That last scene when they're below ground in the shaft, with the rickety stairs that give way. My next thought is for my fellow travelers who aren't super fit, or super young.

Having climbed the stair-tower, we make our way to a narrow wooden platform. We can't go any farther. Above our heads is a rugged shaft rising upward through rough stone. Piling onto the tiny boardwalk takes my breath away. Not in a good way. The smell of bat droppings is enveloping us like an acrid fog. The sweltering humidity makes the smell heavier; several people have pulled their t-shirts up over their mouths and noses. I notice the glistening throats and dripping temples around me and realize I must look the same. Several cell phones are shone upward, disturbing little creatures who awaken with tiny, barely audible shrieks and long wings stretched taut with black skin.

"A Pharaoh named Sneferu built this pyramid sometime between 2,613 and 2,589 BCE," Michael begins, competing for attention with a small black bat swooping above our heads. The bat's sonar-enhanced navigation appears unpredictable and erratic, giving the impression it might fling itself toward any one of us at any moment. After a low fly-by full of what looks like unexpected turbulence, the ebony bat returns to its cavernous abode.

"If you ask a classical Egyptologist, or read textbooks or articles, you will be told that this pyramid was a mistake. That the angle used on the bottom portion proved unstable; the pyramid was cracking, and Sneferu had to alter the slope to complete it," he explained. "But there is another explanation."

That explanation is sacred geometry. In his book *The Divine Blueprint*, author Freddy Silva reveals, "Every temple feels different, partly because of the type of geometry upon which it is based...Each pyramid exerts a different effect on the senses. The [Great] Giza Pyramid's slope angle is based on the seven sided heptagon; the Red Pyramid is based on the pentagon; and the Bent Pyramid reveals the geometries of both the pentagon and hexagon."[14]

Yes, but couldn't the Bent Pyramid have been designed as a hexagonally inspired form, then when it started crumbling, been turned into a pentagonal construction? Maybe. But that doesn't take into account some extraordinary synchronicities. "Geometry is the expression of number in space, thus the pentagon to the hexagon is as 5 is to 6; and of all the planets in our solar system only the Earth incorporates this ratio. It is calculated by taking the 21,600-year period of the obliquity (the tilt of Earth's axis) and dividing it by the precessional cycle of 25,920 years (the wobble at the pole). [The Bent Pyramid] is a metaphor for the balanced relationship between pentagram-based living organisms and hexagon based non-living things...an analog of both planetary and human bodies, and perhaps a point of fusion between them."[15]

---

[14]Silva, Freddy. 2012. *The Divine Blueprint Temples Power Places And The Global Plan to Shape the Human Soul.* Invisible Temple, ME, p. 211.
[15]Ibid.

After an awkward descent back down the wooden tower, we make our way back to the entry point. By which I mean we crouch, crawl, or stoop our way up the same dimly-lit 256-foot stone shaft that brought us here. It's a long haul. I'm about halfway up and closing the gap on an obviously winded woman. Her hike upward has slowed to a step. Grab handrail. Step. Grab handrail. Step. The long periods of inactivity between each movement have me concerned. Remember, this limestone tunnel is three-quarters the length of a football field, angled upwards and hidden deep under many thousands of tons of solid rock. I'm still a ways down but I recognize the khaki-clad bum and white sneakers. She's one of the mature women in our group. I know her as skeptical and standoffish; the few times I've tried to be friendly have only irritated her. I don't even know her name because when I introduced myself she didn't reciprocate. I'm a lifelong athlete and a dance teacher, and I have a lot of energy. I don't want to be the hauling-ass, jacked-up pickup truck whose headlights are right up behind her climbing-as-fast-as-she's-able body.

I stall a bit, taking my time, easing up the shaft as nonchalantly as I can, picking at the limestone walls as if I've found something interesting. Nevertheless, I'm soon just a few yards below Grey Bob. About three feet away, I pause and wait. She's stopped climbing and is crumpled against the shaft wall breathing heavily.

"Are you OK? Do you have water?"

It's ridiculously easy to get dehydrated in the Egyptian desert. I've already seen two tourists collapse from the heat.

"You don't have to stop," she huffs crossly. Her brow

is sprinkled with drops of perspiration like a car windshield in a rainstorm.

I sort of squat down, half kneeling with one leg.

"I have an extra..." I was going to say bottle of water but she doesn't let me finish.

"Just go on!" she hisses, flipping her hand up the shaft, swatting me away like a pesky fly. Then she lowers her eyes and ignores me.

The pinprick sting of her rejection is only a grazing emotional wound. I wonder what happened to make Grey Bob so cynical, so unable to accept my offer of water and compassion? Was it a slow, unconscious slide? Thousands of tiny decisions to settle that eventually carved a deep resentful groove, making interacting with happy people intolerable? Or a sudden and unexpected betrayal that poisoned her heart, from which she hasn't recovered?

I'm incredulous that she's chosen to join this trip— all spirituality, sacred sites, and magic. Not to mention the considerable cost in both money and effort to get oneself not only to the Middle East, but into this claustrophobic subterranean stone trapway deep inside the Bent Pyramid. It's a phenomenal act of strength and adventure for anyone, but Grey Bob seems determined not to enjoy it.

Getting to my feet, I hunch over and step around her, leaving Grey Bob behind in her own shadows. I'm marching powerfully up the wooden floor planks like a fresh pony when she slings a final verbal slap towards my rump.

"Go ahead!," she shouts after me, "you won't be doing that when you're fifty!"

I just keep climbing. I don't have the heart to tell her I'm fifty-five.

***

Outside and above ground, the Bent Pyramid is truly bewitching to behold. Above the flat, empty desert she rises, silent and sacred as a holy mountain. The Bent Pyramid connects to us, if our hearts are light, softly bending our perceptions and our DNA into an altered shape-state. It feels like calmness, acceptance, sanctuary. Why don't they teach us about these places in school? Why don't they teach how the hot wind whistles gently around the pyramids, dancing its invisible dance, while the spirits of the earth and sky, Geb and Nut, embrace in a cosmic coupling that washes electricity through our cells like bioluminescent waves on a nighttime beach?

Walking back to the bus over the sharp rocky sand, many of us have decided to spread out. There is more than enough desert to provide everyone a silent, individual departure from the Bent Pyramid. I am alone on the east side of the monument, out from beneath her immense shadow and nearly free of the structure when a small heartache overcomes me. I feel the thousands of years the Pyramid has stood here, broadcasting her invisible geometric blessing. And how few people ever come close to her. I know it sounds crackers, but the Bent Pyramid seems sad to see me go.

I need to communicate. I must tell the pyramid thank you.

Picking up one of the many stones littering the desert, I give thanks, carving a series of spontaneous symbols into the soft sand. My glyph is 'written' from top to bottom. I do not know these symbols, but I know what they mean and I'm convinced the pyramid will too. Placing several small stones as accent pieces, I stand and declare the sentiment complete. With my heart smiling, I wave farewell to the Bent Pyramid.

By the time I reach the car park, the warm wind has tangled my hair and dried my throat, but as soon as I get a gulp of water, I'm telling my pyramid goodbye story like a teary-eyed teenager talking about a summer crush.

"Here, draw the symbol," Sara hands me a pen and her journal.

When I put the pen to paper I realize I've already forgotten the glyph. Like dream details hovering just beyond memory's reach, I can feel them, but can't translate them. The bus roars to life and boxes of sweet, dried dates are passed down the aisle. Looking back through the wide rear window I watch a bent desert island floating in calm sand seas, getting smaller by the mile.

PART II:

UPPER EGYPT

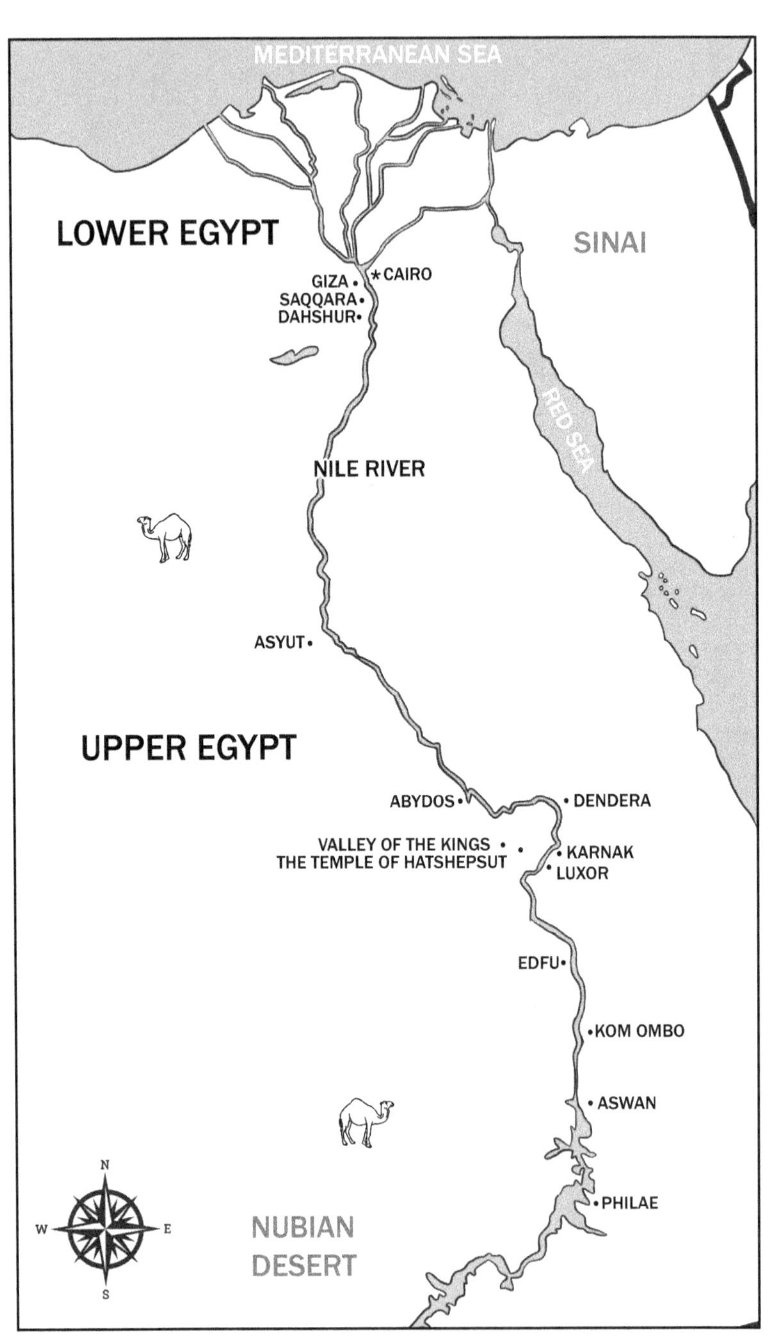

MEDITERRANEAN SEA
LOWER EGYPT
SINAI
GIZA
SAQQARA
DAHSHUR
CAIRO
RED SEA
NILE RIVER
ASYUT
UPPER EGYPT
ABYDOS
DENDERA
VALLEY OF THE KINGS
THE TEMPLE OF HATSHEPSUT
KARNAK
LUXOR
EDFU
KOM OMBO
ASWAN
PHILAE
N
W
E
S
NUBIAN
DESERT

Chapter 8

THE TEMPLE OF HATHOR

When you pass by a highway exit sign that says Nag Hammadi (where the Gnostic Gospels were discovered in 1945) you know it's not just any ordinary day. And indeed it wasn't. Hours earlier, in the domestic departures terminal of Cairo airport, our group boarded a plane bound for Assuit in Upper Egypt. The airport at Sohag—our original destination—was undergoing improvements that prevented our jet from landing there. This meant that instead of a short post-flight transfer to our final destination (Abydos) we were in for an epic road trip across the Egyptian Outback.

I've always loved the desert but even for me the rocky, uninhabited, and seemingly endless wasteland slipping silently by outside the tourist coach windows was slightly unnerving. And the view didn't change. For literally hours. I seriously wondered if a nuclear weapon had been detonated here in ancient times, perhaps as described in the ancient Indian epic the *Mahabharata*. Would I find evidence of vitrified glass pieces if I wandered amongst the sharp rocks and sun-baked sands? That was definitely not an option— maybe not even survivable—in this extreme climate where locals baked round loaves of 'sun bread' by simply setting raw dough balls outside. Like a soul lost in the Duat, our big, bouncy, air-conditioned tourist bus made its way through this topographical dead zone toward the temples of Upper Egypt. Thank Osiris there was a bathroom on board.

Duat—the Otherworld—a place as real to the Egyptians as the physical world. Unlike the physical world…this parallel place exists outside of time; it is present and eternal, and simultaneous with the physical."[16]

Eventually, the not-so-golden sands begin giving way to *beladi* (country) houses, majestic date palm groves, lush irrigated fields, and finally, to a village situated, as is every inhabited spot in Egypt, along a river canal. Like many

---

[16]Silva, Freddy. 2014. *The Lost Art of Resurrection Initiation, Secret Chambers, and the Quest for the Otherworld.* Inner Traditions, Rochester, VT, p.p. 197, 198.

waterways in Egypt, this one is clogged with trash of all kinds. Along the stagnant banks, a defiant white Ibis steps gracefully through plastic debris, poking for food among the rubbish. Here and there an Egyptian boy fishes or wades.

Approaching our hotel, our awkwardly tall motor coach bobbles along the narrow roads that make up the outskirts and inskirts of Abydos, Egypt. Lanky palm fronds and low hanging branches scrape along the top of the bus window before swinging away as we bump along toward our destination. Ubiquitous donkey carts laden high with deep green sugar cane stalks clip along next to us—in living, breathing contrast to our megalithic metal transport. The dark, lean boys and the occasional hijab-covered girl driving the carts wave up at us with wide eyes and friendly grins.

The House of Life Hotel in Abydos, Egypt is named after the Per Ankh, the temples of the ancient Egyptian priest-magicians. People would come to the Per Ankh for physical and psychological healing, or for instruction in the powerful chants and incantations that warded off misfortune and malevolent energies. In the locked libraries of the historical Per Ankh, the priest-magi stored powerful heka—the sacred uses and proper pronunciation of the hieroglyphs. Today, the House of Life hotel in Abydos offers modest but comfortable accommodation and instruction in traditional Egyptian healing and other ritual practices.

I wish I had purchased the *sistrum* (an ancient Egyptian rattle used for music and magic) from the House of Life hotel gift shop but I had barely started browsing when our group was called to the lobby to depart for our next excursion.

"I'll come back for this," I told the gentle Egyptian shopkeeper.

"*Inshallah*," he answered with a smile.

Inshallah is a common phrase in Egypt, which means "if God wills it to happen." Traditionally used as a serious and sincere expression of hope, its use has become increasingly ubiquitous and casual.

Once again I find myself watching through the immense coach windows as the locals go about their daily lives. The bus bobbles its way back out of town and onto the gravel road that leads through a small series of hills and valleys to Dendera, the Temple of the Goddess Hathor.

Hathor is the goddess of dance, music, drunkenness, adornment, and sexuality, as well as a tutelary deity of motherhood and children. Worshipped for thousands of years as a primordial sky goddess, Hathor predates the cult of Isis, with whom she is frequently confused. Often depicted in the form of a cow, Hathor appears in human form with small cow ears. Mistress of the Stars, Hathor was said to be the daughter of Nut, the sky, and the sun god Ra. Beautiful Hathor can be identified in temple reliefs and artwork by her headdress—a sun disk uplifted by two cow horns. Depictions of Queen Isis, in contrast, show her wearing a chair headdress—symbolic of the throne of Egypt.

Hathor arrived in Egypt from her homeland to the southeast, a mysterious land called Punt. Punt was a magical place, where coveted Myrrh trees grew and lions and ostriches roamed. Perhaps it was located on the coastline of Somalia or in the Arabian Peninsula. It's possible that Hathor hailed from the fertile crescent of Mesopotamia, where she was known as the Sumerian goddess Ninhursag, caught between the conflicting campaigns of her two half-brothers, the ancient Sumerian Lords Enki and Enlil (possibly known in Egypt as Osiris and Set.)

Hat-hor means House of Horus, and indeed, she is said to have been the consort of Horus, but Hathor can also be translated as "my house is the sky."[17] Could Hathor have been one of the long-lived Anunnaki from Sumeria, a daughter or descendant of Anu? These prehistoric space travelers, known as the Anunna, are likely the Watchers in the Christian Bible and the Shining Ones in many ancient myths. In several ancient cuneiform stone tablets such as the Atrahasis, Hathor (under her Sumerian name Ninhursag or Ninmah) is credited, along with her brother Enki, with genetically engineering Homo sapiens sapiens. The ancient Mesopotamian word for Earth is Ki, and so the Anunnaki were the Anunna who descended to Ki (Earth). Ninhursag/ Hathor was also called Mama Ki, literally Mother Earth.[18]

The idea that the Egyptian Hathor and Sumerian Ninmah are one and the same deity is supported in many ways, such as Hathor's depiction as a nurturing mother, often

---

[17]Bleeker, C.J. 1973. *Hathor and Thoth: Two Key Figures of the Ancient Egyptian Religion.* Brill, p.p. 25, 48.

[18]Mark, Joshua J. 2017. *Ninhursag* (https://worldhistory.org/ Ninhursag). Accessed on August 19, 2022

nursing important personages. In the temple of Hatshepsut near the Valley of the Kings, there is a special area dedicated to Hathor. Statues, carvings, and paintings from other temples show a human Hathor nursing youngsters, always from her left breast. Similarly, Early Sumerian rulers liked to describe themselves as "constantly nourished by Ninhursag with milk."[19]

Approaching the Dendera temple through the vast courtyard one can't help but wonder at the scale of the thing. Like many Egyptian temples, the architecture seems made for giants. Immense doorways and massive hieroglyph-covered columns dwarf modern tourists. On the top of the fifty-six foot tall sandstone pillars that form the front façade of Dendera's hypostyle hall, six gigantic carved faces of Hathor welcomed followers of the Old Religion as recently as 300 BCE.

Today, those faces are gouged out.

It's a shock to discover how many stone carvings of the gods and goddesses up and down the Nile are defaced, chiseled away in a very deliberate manner. The truth is, no one really knows who carried this out, or why. One explanation is that the early Muslims or Coptic Christians destroyed the art in an attempt to invalidate the Old Religion, or more likely to remove the occult power and information they feared was somehow retained in the stone carvings. Curiously, many of the defacements are bewilderingly specific. The face of one goddess may be precisely chipped away while the neter next to her is left untouched. Passionate zealots bent on righteous

---

[19]Kramer, S.N. 1977. *The Sumerians: Their History, Culture and Character.* University of Chicago Press.

violence are not prone to such assiduous selection. Similarly, portions of stone hieroglyphics on temple walls up and down the Nile have been found painstakingly redacted—while adjacent portions remain intact. This would necessitate the ability to "read" the hieroglyphs and determine the offending content, a skill which neither historical Christians nor Muslims possessed.

One theory is that the Egyptians themselves chipped out the representations of sacred personages and hieroglyphs that did, in fact, encode the mysteries and magic of their culture, to prevent the *heka* (magic) from being misused in future times.

The magic may have been chiseled from the stone faces, but the land upon which the temples stand—and some say the stone buildings themselves—are still alive, waiting to enchant the sensitive visitor. Dendera is said to be one of the original 'primordial mounds,' places selected and consecrated by the neters (gods) themselves during Zep Tepi, the ancient Egyptian term for the First Time or Genesis. These sites include Giza, Karnak, Luxor, Dendera, Edfu, and Kom Ombo, all precisely sited on telluric and geomagnetic matrices.

What are telluric and geomagnetic matrices? According to Wikipedia, A telluric current (from Latin tellūs, "earth"), or Earth current, is an electric current which moves underground or through the sea. Telluric currents result from both natural causes and human activity, and the discrete currents interact in a complex pattern.

Regarding geomagnetism, the U.S. National Oceanic and Atmospheric Administration (NOAA) website explains,

"The geomagnetic field measured at any point on the Earth's surface is a combination of several magnetic fields generated by various sources. These fields are superimposed on and interact with each other. More than 90% of the field measured is generated INTERNAL to the planet in the Earth's outer core."[20]

Were the ancient gods able to identify locations that were tellurically and geomagnetically gifted, or did they possess the ability to converge these energies to their will? If so, who were these gods?

The ancient myths are clear on the fact that the gods Hathor and Horus were lovers, and that they had a child together named Ihy. Horus is well known as the offspring of Isis and Osiris and is often depicted as a broad-shouldered man with a falcon's head. Horus was conceived when Isis used her magic to temporarily revive her murdered husband long enough to receive his essence, though the holy (or scientific) details of that fecundating process are not fully explained. The confusion arises because of some ancient references to an "elder" Horus, leading to speculation that there may have been more than one god named Horus. The family tree of the ancient Egyptian pantheon is a dense thicket, with branches spliced and entwined in ways that challenge modern mores. Isis and Osiris, for example, are brother and sister and husband and wife, as are their siblings Nephthys and Set. If these supernatural personalities were more than archetypes—perhaps some kind of advanced humanoid or even people from other areas of the galaxy—their lifespans may have been significantly longer, no doubt confounding

---

[20]NOAA. *Geomagnetism* (nddc.noaa.gov/geomag). Accessed on August 19, 2022.

historians attempting to document lineages.

The ancients describe the neters as extremely tall, somewhat human looking people that arrived after the great flood to assist humanity, procreating among themselves before mysteriously disappearing to parts unknown. Long after they left the land of Khem, the sacred coupling of the neters was reenacted as religious ritual up and down the Nile. Once a year, the Festival of Hathor was held at Dendera, after which her statue was floated down the Nile on a barque to be reunited with the representation of her beloved, the falcon-headed god Horus at his Edfu temple.

I imagine the lilting music and exotic drumbeats that greeted the revelers gathered here to honor Hathor. It is accepted that many guests arrived by boat, for at the time this temple was in use the Nile flowed just outside the earthen perimeter wall. After disembarking, visiting villagers as well as gods and goddesses from other parts of Khemet would ascend a series of smooth megalithic stone steps. Standing frozen in the hot breeze, with Ra roughing my cheeks, my mind's eye is recreating just such a scene. On each step stands a priest to the right and a priestess to the left, creating a stunning visual—a human pyramid of sorts. The priests are bare chested, sporting stiff white kilts and holding the tethers of large, once-wild cats (caracals, cheetahs, and at times, lions). The priestesses wear long, slim-fitting dresses with patterns that resembled iridescent fish scales or glittering stars. The body-skimming gowns rise to a band which encircles the upper rib cage, exposing their breasts and upper back. Each priestess dons a single, supple leather gauntlet upon which is perched an elegant falcon wearing gilded leather jesses. Unlike the stony-faced sentinels of today's royal courts, the welcome committee smiles warmly at each attendee, for it is their job to ensure every person arriving feels like family returning. And indeed they were, for at that time, the blood of the gods still flowed inside many humans.

Inside the courtyard incense wafts, sistrums jingle and zills clip along in rhythms still heard in Egyptian shisha bars today. Enormous billowing curtains create lounging areas where priestesses in golden dresses dance sacred shapes through the colorful carpets and into the earth below. Then using their bodies, they spiral the energy back to the heavens, their gold-banded arms raised in ecstasy. The plentiful food and drink is served on golden platters adorned with images of beautiful hawk-headed men. Visitors—both men and women—wear their very best clothing, line their eyes with kohl and have perfumed their bodies and hair with fragrant oils. Flowing dresses and skirts of the finest white Egyptian cotton are belted with golden girdles, or for the men, colorful sashes. High Sem Priestesses—identified by their leopard skin garments—bless babies, lovers, and mothers with healing spells, stones, and herbs. Above all of this, the seated statue of Hathor looks down on the celebration with a mother's unconditional love.

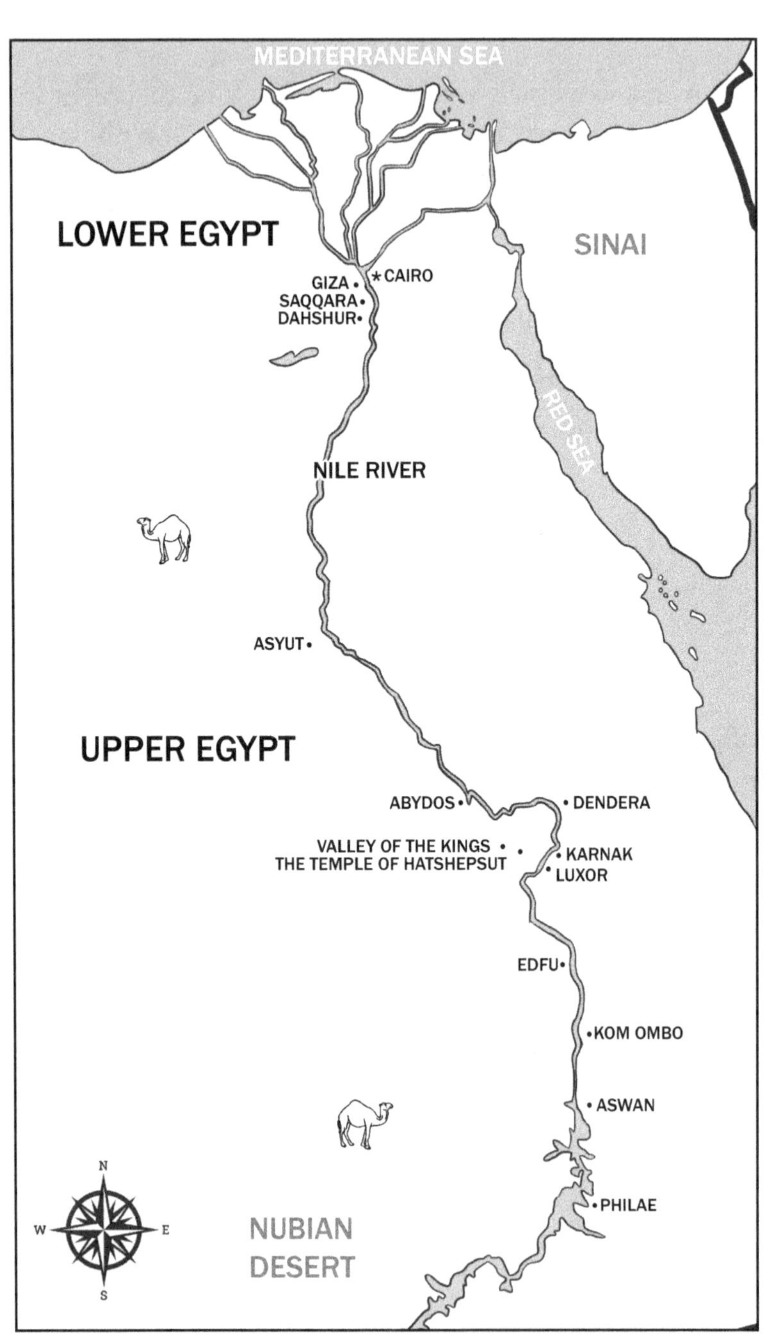

MEDITERRANEAN SEA
LOWER EGYPT
SINAI
GIZA
SAQQARA
DAHSHUR
* CAIRO
RED SEA
NILE RIVER
ASYUT
UPPER EGYPT
ABYDOS
DENDERA
VALLEY OF THE KINGS
THE TEMPLE OF HATSHEPSUT
KARNAK
LUXOR
EDFU
KOM OMBO
ASWAN
PHILAE
NUBIAN
DESERT
N
W
E
S

Chapter 9

THE
DENDERA
LIGHTBULB

I'm still processing the sheer magnitude of Dendera, from the impossibly tall sixty-foot walls and columns to the many individual chapel rooms—all covered from floor to soaring ceiling with exquisite carvings and colorful paintings—when our guide announces what I've been waiting for: We are going to the Dendera lightbulb!

For those who haven't heard of it, this thought-provoking artwork is located in a once-secret room beneath the stone floor of the Temple.

The only access to the subterranean chamber is through a very small square opening in the stone floor through which one must drop down and wriggle through. When the time came that we were allowed down the rabbit hole, I was the first in line! One of the officials motions to the opening and holds out his hand, I accept his leathered palm with a shukren and am lowered in. I am thankful to be wearing yoga pants under my long dress, which does not descend as gracefully as I do! Once underneath the temple floor, I proceed forward through the exceedingly narrow stone hallway. Behind me, the rest of the group has dropped in and queued up, filling the cramped subterranean tunnel with a hum of activity and bodies—and physically eliminating any possibility of changing my mind and turning back.

I lead the group forward until the tunnel ends at a decorated stone wall—a "T" in the passageway. To the right and left, two steps descend into a corridor perpendicular to the one in which we stand.

"Which way is the lightbulb?" asks the woman just behind me.

"It's this way," I reply, despite the fact that this is my first visit to Egypt and I have certainly never been beneath the floor of Dendera temple. Turning intuitively to the left, I dash down the steps and into an even deeper and more claustrophobic corridor.

At the dead end of this narrow, tomblike tunnel is where one must go to see the controversial wall carving. The bas relief depicts Egyptian men holding what looks like an enormous incandescent lightbulb, complete with a stylized serpent filament and a lotus bud base, to which a 'power

The Dendera "Lightbulb"

cord' is attached. Some ancient alien theorists speculate that the carving is literal; that the ancient monuments may have actually been illuminated with electrical style lighting. Others propose the scene alludes to the location being used for 'living resurrection' ceremonies, induced by sensory deprivation, meditation (and perhaps some hallucinogenic blue lotus plants). On the opposite wall an additional 'lightbulb' tableau is depicted. Caressing the fine bas relief, I am struck by how intricately carved and smoothly polished they are. The scenes here are also a darker, warmer color than those in the above-ground sandstone temple. I later learn this is because they are carved from a megalithic slab of limestone purposefully buried beneath the floor of the temple as a canvas.

I could stay here forever, staring at the gorgeous goddesses and handsome falcons that decorate Dendera's subterranean chamber. What an art gallery! Having been a Master Falconer, I appreciate the anatomical accuracy of the birds, complete with killing tooth and primary feather tips crossed behind their backs. Whoever carved these raptors had an intimate knowledge of falcon anatomy and behaviour. But the tiny space is getting ever more crowded. And humid. Some people are trying to take flash pictures. Due to the low ceiling, the tall people can't even stand up straight.

I retreat against a wall, my back pressed into a priceless stone carving, then make a break for it. Since the subterranean space won't fit two humans passing side by side, I do the party twist through the gaggle of perspiring people, navigating back to the entrance and eventually climbing back up through the floor and into the temple proper.

Chapter 10

AN UNLIKELY MAGI

I am astonished to have many of the rooms and passageways of Dendera temple to myself today. The tourists have not yet returned to Egypt and the majestic footprint of the complex allows visitors to disperse into empty chapels and disappear behind massive columns. I'm standing alone inside a windowless stone room, one of the many extensively carved and decorated chapels inside Dendera temple, craning my neck to admire an elaborate painted border along the top of the walls. It takes a moment before I realize I'm looking at hundreds of realistically rendered cobras side by side. Their flared yellow hoods barely touch their neighbors, creating a stylish and literally striking design. Farther in, a particularly beautiful section of the back wall draws my gaze: a broad-shouldered, hawk-headed man steps forward in bas relief, his arm reaching back to clasp the delicate hand of a naked goddess. As I stare, the carved edges of their arms and legs seem to morph into three-dimensions. Cocking my head, I notice the realistic soft pouch of their taut stomachs punctuated by the natural depressions of their perfect belly buttons. It's as if I'm looking at a black and white art photograph come to life. Moving closer, I trace the edges of their stone bodies with my hand, as if to convince myself of their inanimacy. Yet the moment I step back, they again seem to inflate from their stone canvas into three dimensions. What art technique or sorcery created this effect? I don't have time to ponder it because an angular Egyptian man has approached, beckoning me to follow him.

He coaxes me non-verbally, as one would a puppy, out through the giant sized stone doorway and down the hall to the adjacent, end-most chapel. Of course I've got my guard up; I'm unsure of his intentions. But it's broad daylight and I can hear the voices of other tourists nearby, and frankly, he doesn't look or feel the least bit dangerous in his faded galabeya and flimsy sandals. I notice his dark toes are coated with the temple sands. He seems to indicate he's got a secret to share, and my curiosity gets the better of me. What effects might a living temple have on a person who visits almost every day, marinating, even unconsciously, in her embedded initiatory effects? What secrets would she reveal, and who would you share those secrets with?

Once we're inside, he proceeds to the left rear point of the chapel and backs himself into the masonry corner, closing his eyes and clasping his hands in a prayerful pose. Then he opens his eyes and looks up at the opposite wall. Pointing his fingers at his eyes and then back at the spot on the wall, he looks to see if I understand. I nod and start to walk away—I'm not really sure what is happening at this point.

"No, no, no," he coos and points toward the corner.

Alright. I'll go and stand in the corner. Apparently, I'm being put in some kind of Egyptian time-out. The absurdity of the scene is almost making me giggle. I'm not quite in the right spot, however, for my friend again feels the need to demonstrate, pressing his back against the stone corner. I try again, and seem to meet his approval. He points at his eyes and closes them, again, taking a meditative pose.

I'm not sure I want to have my eyes closed all alone with this Egyptian stranger. He seems to read my mind, for he backs away to the far wall in a submissive posture to indicate his harmlessness. I close my eyes.

The ancient stone is pressing sharply into my shoulder blades from both sides of the 90 degree stone angle I'm wedged into, perspiration is running down my chest from the ungodly heat, my backpack is tucked behind my legs to deter any potential pick–pocketing, and nevertheless, I feel myself almost instantly drop into a deep meditative state. After a few minutes I open my eyes and the fellow moves toward me, indicating I should look at the opposite wall, which I do. He points again; I'm not quite staring where he intends. Following his outstretched arm, my gaze ascends to the apparent area of interest. And then it starts.

The stone floor of the chapel begins gently rocking forward and back. I watch as the wall carvings rise and fall, as if they are on the opposite side of my seesaw. I'm not feeling the least bit dizzy or lightheaded, it's just that the whole room is moving! I press myself deeper into the chapel corner to immobilize my body, but the rock under my feet just keeps rolling. After a time, the waves dissipate to a soft buzz inside my cells. My Egyptian friend approaches with a big smile, then presents his open palm, making the universal sign for money. It takes me a moment to realize he's asking for backsheesh. I fumble through my pocketbook for an Egyptian bill, which disappears from my fingers the moment it's offered. Then out the door he sweeps, never to be seen again.

I rejoin my tour group underneath the Dendera Zodiac, which is on the temple ceiling in an area dedicated to the god Osiris. The exact age of the zodiac is disputed, but all agree it is very ancient. The artistic circular carving represents the 360 day Egyptian year. The twelve constellations of the zodiac are depicted, along with thirty six organizing decans- -three for each sign.

"The original is in a museum in Paris, it was blasted out of the temple by an antiquities dealer in Napoleonic times..." Michael is explaining.

I'm missing most of what must be a fascinating education about this extraordinary planisphere. My body is still buzzing and I'm wondering what just happened?

Chapter 11

AVENUE OF THE SPHINXES

Today we continue to explore Upper Egypt, which is actually to the south when looking at a map of the region. The Nile flows downward from its highest location in the Nubian desert (what is now Sudan) toward Lower Egypt (where Cairo, Giza, and Heliopolis are located) to finally become the Nile Delta, spreading like a cobra's hood into the Mediterranean. The famous city of Alexandria is located in the Nile Delta.

We are four-hundred miles up the Nile from Giza,

where an extravagant three kilometer promenade flanked by stone sphinxes originally linked the Karnak temple complex to Luxor temple. In ancient times this area was called Thebes. Today, quite a few beautifully preserved sphinxes remain in place at both temple entrances, and there is a project in the works to restore the entire 1.5 mile boulevard and its hundreds of sphinxes. These aren't colossal carvings like the Sphinx of Giza, but stately statues of a more modern proportion. One day, visitors may again be able to stroll between the two open-air temples. What a walk that will be! But there is work to do. Traveling by bus to Karnak, I peer over a highway overpass railing and glimpse priceless ancient sphinxes half reclaimed by roadside vegetation or partially buried, still guarding their long-abandoned avenue between the temples. Closer to the monuments, the sphinxes receive their proper respect, cordoned off from climbing children and overzealous selfie takers.

The sphinxes flanking the approach to Luxor have human heads, while those decorating the Karnak plaza sport beautiful ram heads atop lion bodies.

The ram was the symbol of the Egyptian god Amun, an ancient sky god, or neter, who rose to preeminence in the Twelfth Dynasty (1991 BCE–1786 BCE). Amun (or Amen) is the great unseen energy that pervades and sustains all creation—what today we might call the quantum field or Divine Matrix. Karnak was Amun's primary place of veneration.

In the temples of Karnak and Luxor, Amun is represented as a blue-skinned man wearing a distinctive double-plumed headdress. Isn't it interesting that Amun, a primordial Egyptian creator god, and the Hindu creator god

Vishnu are both depicted as blue-skinned?

Vishnu, like Amun, is considered the creator of all things and the guardian of creation. In Sanskrit, Vishnu translates as "all pervasive."[21] According to Medhātith (circa 1,000 CE), Vishnu is "one who is everything and inside everything."[22] In *The Passion of Isis and Osiris*, Author Jean Houston describes the Egyptian god Amun: "He was called He Who Abides in All Things, and he becomes the essence of soul or ba. His name abides even on the lips of Christians who end their prayers by intoning his name 'Amen.' "

---

[21] Swami Chinmayananda. *Translation of Vishnu Sahasranama.* Central Chinmaya Mission Trust, Mumbai, p.p. 16-17.

[22] Klostermaier, Klaus. 2000. *Hinduism: A Short History.* Oneworld Publications, p.p. 83-84.

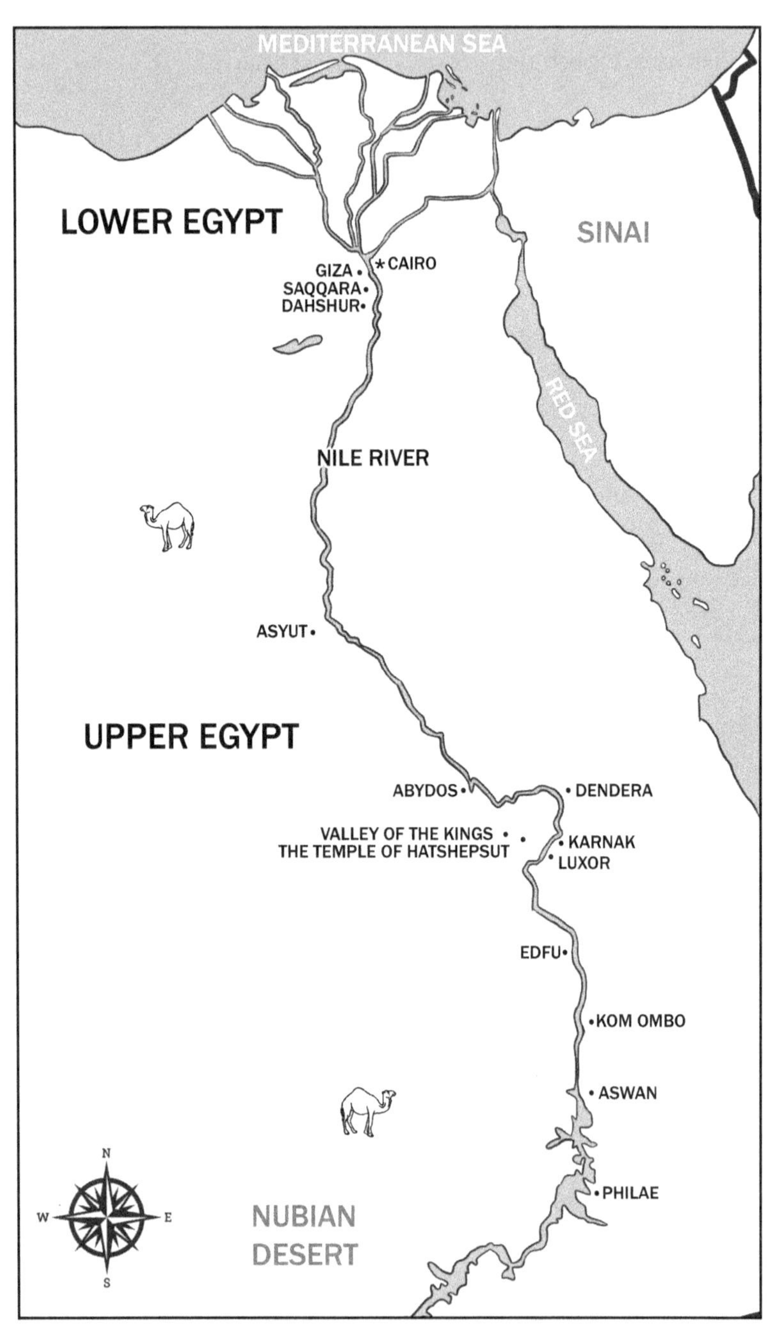

MEDITERRANEAN SEA
LOWER EGYPT
SINAI
GIZA
SAQQARA
DAHSHUR
CAIRO
RED SEA
NILE RIVER
ASYUT
UPPER EGYPT
ABYDOS
DENDERA
VALLEY OF THE KINGS
THE TEMPLE OF HATSHEPSUT
KARNAK
LUXOR
EDFU
KOM OMBO
ASWAN
PHILAE
NUBIAN
DESERT
N
W
E
S

Chapter 12

KARNAK

The Karnak temple complex is located on the east bank of the Nile River in Upper Egypt, in a place historically called Thebes but today is the modern city of Luxor. Karnak is one of the largest ceremonial centers ever built, covering about 200 acres. Countless buildings and shrines, towering pylons and obelisks, and a large rectangular lake are among the varied architectural elements that comprise this sacred site, which the ancient Egyptians called Ipet-isut, "The Most Selected of Places."

I have been handed back my torn entry ticket and flow with the air conditioning through the interpretive center. After a short detour into the ladies' room, I continue on toward the welcome center's pièce de résistance; a vast and intricately detailed architect's model of the ancient sprawl that is Karnak.

The grounds are so large that the model requires a huge display table under whose glass top stands a complete reproduction of the Karnak complex, rendered in tiny but impressive detail.

"Come over here," I suggest to Sara, walking around the left hemisphere of the table to stake out a spot on the far side of the display. Our group has started circling the diorama and I want to get a good look at it.

Soon Michael strides up and around the right side of the display, taking a position directly to my left, addressing those assembled.

"This," he waves his arm with a dramatic flourish over the miniature Ipet–Isut, "is Karnak Temple."

"It's smaller than I expected, " I quip.

"You remind me of Star Wars," he laughs, clearly amused, before quoting Anakin Skywalker from *Episode III: Return of the Sith*. "General Grievous. You're shorter than I expected."

Michael is pointing out the various sections of the temple on the scale model and explaining the plan. It's impossible to see all of Karnak in one day—or even several days—but we will see some of the most important architecture and our Egyptian Guide Shani wants to share a special chapel with us. After that, we can choose to wander at will, although Michael will be leading a group to the sacred lake for anyone who wants to join.

Then we push our way through the rear glass doors of the interpretive center and walk down a wide stone avenue. A line of exquisite, ram-headed sphinxes watch from both sides of the promenade as we make our way toward and through Karnak temple's stupendous first, and then second, pylon.

Moments ago we seemed like giant gods ourselves, overlooking the Lilliputian rendering of Karnak in the interpretive area. Now, entering the 3,300 year old Great Hypostyle Hall, the tables have turned.

Years of Darwinian conditioning shatter like glass against twelve immensely massive columns reaching like old-growth, sandstone Sequoias to the architraves seventy-five feet above. The remaining rows of pillars tower a mere forty feet or so above the dehydrated mortals who linger gratefully in their shadows. Slatted stone panels still perch atop the structure; the remnants of clerestory windows that provided daylight to the 50,000 square foot area when it was still covered by its flat stone roof. The majestic carved columns represent stylized papyrus stalks. Some flare into bloom at the top and others remain as buds, but all are carved round and vertically with pharaohs and falcons and cheeky cobras wearing the tall crown of Upper Egypt. Cartouches, ankhs, and anatomically impressive moths share the huge rotund stone canvases with slender goddesses, sacred bulls, and Benu birds. A detailed chapter of humanity that most of us were never taught in school is carved in deep relief as far as the eye can see, but it goes casually unnoticed by the visitors using the gigantic pedestal bases as resting places. They look like toddlers seated on tall chairs, their feet dangling a foot or two above the ancient temple floor as they check their cell phones and cameras, leaning back against the legacies of the gods themselves.

Further into the temple rises an obelisk that Queen Hatshepsut erected, its tip piercing the sapphire sky seventy-five feet above me. The refined phallus is fashioned from a single chunk of pink granite of between 350 and 700 tons. Bewilderingly, this stone was quarried from Aswan, which is hundreds of miles to the south. No one knows exactly how it was transported to Karnak. The pointy topmost portion—what is called the pyramidion—was originally encased in precious metal: gold, silver, or an alloy of the two called electrum. Was this obelisk a glittering statement of Queen Hatshepsut's success (she raised another two obelisks to commemorate her sixteenth year as Pharaoh) or some kind of Pharaonic Tesla tower? Granite contains a significant amount of quartz, which is used today in much of our advanced technology; it's in every computer chip. One can only marvel at the amount of data that could be stored in this pink granite hard drive.

In *The Passion of Isis and Osiris*, Jean Houston reveals "The ancient Egyptians had no doubt that the images of the neters were alive...the living statue of a god also contained that god's visionary powers and the ability to know what existed in the durative realm...The statues in the temples were the earthly residences for the neters."[23]

---

[23]Houston, Jean. 1995. *The Passion of Isis and Osiris*. Ballantine/ Wellspring (Random House), NY, p. 168.

Incorporating the living energy of the gods into their likenesses carved in stone seems superstitious, silly, or downright spooky, but not seriously possible. At least that's what I thought until I entered a small chapel on the outskirts of Karnak and came face to face with the lion-headed goddess Sehkmet.

She was human–size, standing behind a small barrier rope, left foot forward in the classic stance, her lioness head facing forward. And she was looking at me. Her stone eyelids weren't blinking, her black granite body wasn't moving, yet there was an overwhelming sense of sentience coming from the statue. The energy—her personality—was forceful, magnetic, and direct. And it was palpable, not just to me, but to the majority of women in the group who crowded forward to stare into her eyes, captivated, as I was, by her countenance. She wasn't threatening, but she did seem to initiate the contact and it was strangely difficult to break away from her stare. The strength of this warrior goddess feels both comforting and protective. Not simply a mindless weapon wielded by Ra, Sekhmet struck me as a neter in her own right—a bad-ass lioness in a black granite jacket.

I stood back by the door to allow additional ladies their communion with the idol, watching them exit afterward with smiles and tear-stained cheeks. One woman who was troubled by a recent personal tragedy came out of the shrine with the lines on her face smoothed away and looking several decades younger!

Shani was waiting for us as we exited, silent and knowing. Once everyone was accounted for, she led us back to a more central meeting point, a wall that I recognized. We had walked by it on the way to Sekhmet's shrine.

Shani and Michael are up against the wall and he is leaning down to better hear her. Then he gestures toward the wall. "See these grooves?" Michael asks the group, pointing to smooth looking vertical slashes running the length of the wall. "These are from soldiers sharpening their swords before going into battle."

I want to ask what battle and what Dynasty. Were these Queen Hatshepsut's warriors, whom she is said to have assisted with sorcery? Or Nubian, Roman, or Greek soldiers?

"I'm taking a group to the sacred lake," Michael announces, striding away, pulling most of the group with him.

"If you prefer to explore on your own, you must be back at the bus by 3:30 p.m." Shani warns loudly.

I would love to see the enormous rectangular lake, but I can't get something out of my mind. We often get a primer on the day's monuments en-route, and today's talk included a recommendation to visit the Alabaster Chapel at Karnak.

"Shani, I want to go see the Alabaster Chapel."

"Okay," she says, adjusting her red sun parasol, which is not only for UV protection, but helps us locate her in the crowded monuments, "I will walk you part of the way there."

As the majority of the group traipse off to the sacred lake, Shani and I head in the opposite direction, back toward the front of the temple where the Alabaster Chapel is located. We walk in friendly, comfortable silence along oven-hot paths lined with rock rubble and scented with the layered notes of a very subtle perfume: desert sand, very old stone, and exotic smells I don't recognize.

Shani sees me looking at the stones.

"These are the blocks they haven't put back into place for the restoration of the temple," Shani explains.

Among the sandstone boulders used to delineate the walking trail for visitors is a large block carved with a cobra and a falcon. The bottom of the rock has been broken off but the heads are clearly visible. The cobra wears the tall crown of Upper Egypt. The falcon wears the combined crown of Upper and Lower Egypt. Only one god wears this double crown: Horus.

Shani smiles and indulges me as I stop to take a picture of the block. Anywhere else in the world, this authentic, ancient carved stone might be a museum's cherished display; here it is relegated to walkway edging.

"Okay Beautiful, just walk that way until you get to the Open Air Museum. You will have to buy a ticket."

Shani has taken on a mothering role to all of us in the group, although I think she and I may be about the same age.

"Be back at the bus by 3:30."

"I will. I promise."

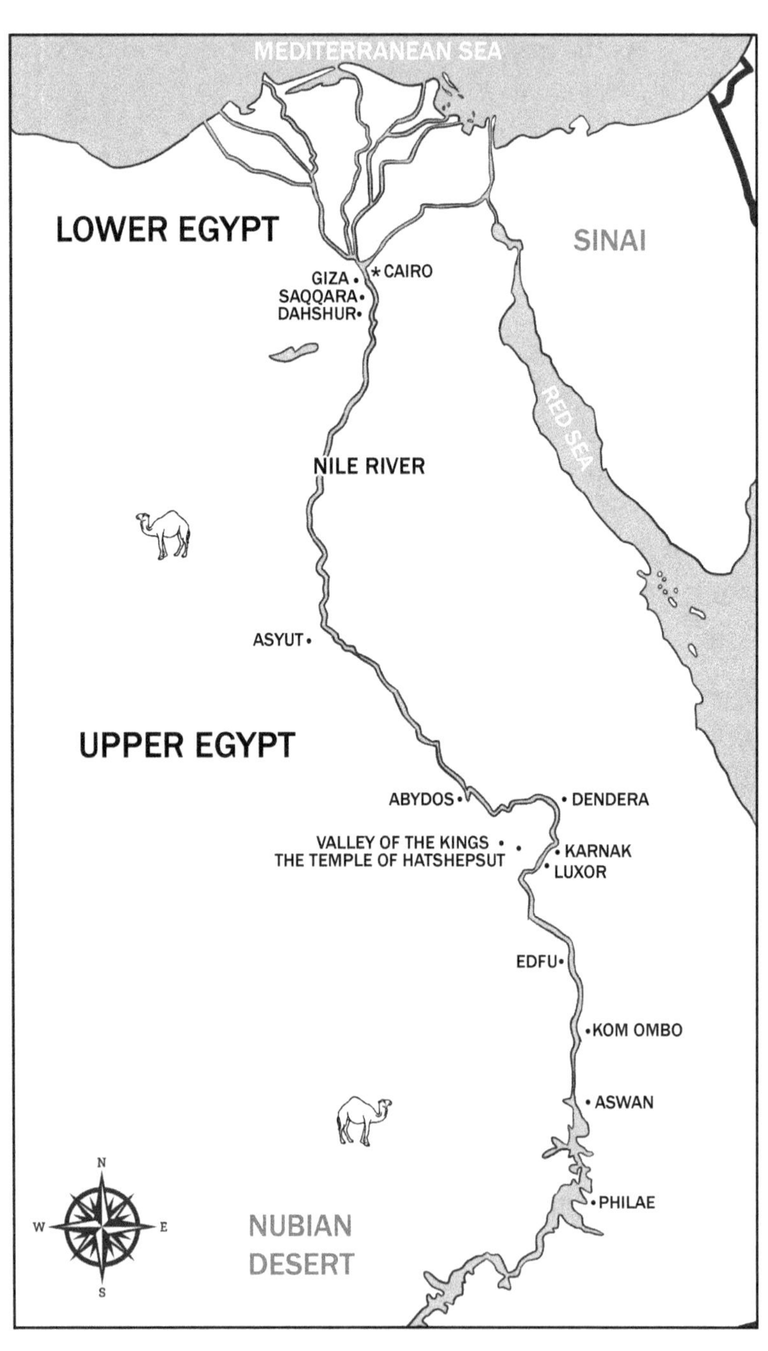

MEDITERRANEAN SEA
LOWER EGYPT
SINAI
GIZA
SAQQARA
DAHSHUR
CAIRO
RED SEA
NILE RIVER
ASYUT
UPPER EGYPT
ABYDOS
DENDERA
VALLEY OF THE KINGS
THE TEMPLE OF HATSHEPSUT
KARNAK
LUXOR
EDFU
KOM OMBO
ASWAN
PHILAE
NUBIAN
DESERT
N
S
E
W

Chapter 13

THE OPEN AIR MUSEUM AT KARNAK

The Alabaster Chapel is located in the Open Air Museum at Karnak, which is simply another area of the temple complex near the front. Unlike the rest of Karnak, however, the Open Air Museum features a shaded grove of mature trees. I've been told this section requires an additional entry fee and I've located a sign and a small wooden ticket kiosk, but it's closed and locked. There isn't a soul in sight anywhere.

"Hello," I call into the dark window, but only the breeze

replies. I peer around the back of the building. Nothing. I've just about decided to head up the gravel path anyway—there's no barrier of any kind—when a plump Egyptian woman in a long dress and heavy hijab comes bustling up the path.

"I want to see the Alabaster Chapel," I explain, "How much is a ticket?"

The woman seems extremely flustered by my presence. She tries to open the door to the ticket booth but it's locked. I try to hand her some money, but she shakes her head. She's saying something in Arabic which I don't understand.

I try to communicate a low-stress vibe, "Is this where I get the ticket?"

"OK" she says in English, smiling. "Ticket."
We both know she's stalling.

We see him at the same time, the husky, fifty-ish Egyptian gentleman strolling up the gravel path. The woman is visibly relieved and for some reason, I get the impression that they're husband and wife. He's wearing a white button down shirt with the sleeves rolled up, dark trousers, and black leather belt.

"You want a ticket?" He asks, as if there might be some other reason I'm waiting here on the edge of Karnak temple in front of this neter-forsaken little entry kiosk.

"Yes, to see the Alabaster Chapel. How much is a ticket?"

He's unlocking the wooden door. "Forty pounds."

It seems kind of high, but not exorbitant.

"Okay," I deftly retrieve two twenty-pound Egyptian bills out of my backpack.

By now he's into the kiosk and ruffling around. There seems to be a problem. Hubby and wife exchange some very fast Arabic and then Mr. Ticket Man walks quickly away, down the gravel path toward the main temple.

"Where's he going?" I ask.

"Tickets," the woman says, flipping on an old-fashioned wire desk fan and offering me the only chair inside the sweltering little casket of a kiosk. Once inside I am happy to see a few accoutrements that indicate this is, in fact, a ticket booth. Oh why did I wear this full skirt today? My thighs are damp from perspiration under the yards of linen and when I peel my forearm off the vinyl chair a wet image of it remains. I can actually feel my temperature rising. My keeper senses I'm moments from an abrupt departure and produces a chilled bottle of water from a cleverly concealed refrigerator.

"Shukren," (Thank you) I respond in Egyptian Arabic, pressing it to my shiny forehead before twisting it open.

"Afwan," she smiles.

The small blades of the fan are a futile gesture against the mighty heat of Upper Egypt. We sit in silence. My keeper must be cooking in her full-length dress and head covering but if so, she doesn't show it. I can't take it anymore, the awkward, sweating silence. Water or no water, I'm leaving!

I'm rising in the cramped space toward the open door when Mr. Ticket Man returns. Relief floods my psyche, as refreshing as a rainshower on a humid summer afternoon.

He produces the ticket. I hand him the bills.

"Sixty pounds," he says.

We all know he said forty when he left. Nevertheless, I pull out another 20-pound note cheerfully. I'm just so glad things are moving forward. The whole ticket is less than a Starbucks at home and the Egyptian people have been especially hard hit by the crash of the tourism industry.

The transaction finally completed, I resume my walk up the dirt path to the ancient garden. The area is littered with leaves, additional temple bits and more damaged blocks, but the grounds immediately surrounding the structures are impeccably neat and tidy. What looks like fine French gravel borders the buildings and above them billowing branches of mature trees expand skyward like deep green thunderheads. And not a single other human for as far as the eye can see.

I enter the Alabaster Chapel, the Chapel of Pharaoh Amenhotep I, which is a small rectangular building with tall door openings on both short sides. Intended as a sanctuary for the sacred *barque* (boat) of Amen (Amun-Ra), it was originally built by Amenhotep I between 1525 and 1504 BCE. Queen Hatshepsut enhanced the structure circa 1479-1458 BCE, though it was later destroyed by her stepson, rival, and heir, Thutmose III. It was only recently reconstructed in 1947, by matching up the carvings on the scattered stone blocks like a jigsaw puzzle.

It is difficult to describe the feeling of gentle and profound clarity that results from standing inside a small room made entirely and exclusively of huge blocks of pure alabaster. I place my hands upon the carved scenes, tracing the wavy variations of color: ivory to caramel to the faintest peach. Queen Hatshepsut may have touched this very stone, or even Amenhotep I, so long, long ago. I think of the god Amun, for whom this chapel was made. He of the double-plumbed headdress, blue skin, and stylish beard. I would love to know who—or what—he really was. How odd that after thinking of something, my mind does not continue to jump around connecting tangent dots, but returns to me like a pristine white gyrfalcon. A light breeze dances through the chapel, like the touch of angels, and I feel an idea. I begin to sing. Not a song, or even words, just tones as they come to me, rising and falling as they wish. And here's the thing. I'm not a singer. I'm really not. But these sounds are the most beautiful I've ever heard.

At first I can't believe they are coming from me! Some kind of supernatural stone acoustics are taking my simple sounds and turning them into what I can only describe as angelic whale song. I experiment with very high notes, which rise like liquid crystal before I let them fall into sonic waves that wash like audible starlight around the chapel. I stand alone for a long time, playfully absorbing the vibrations of my own transfigured voice. It was only after I walked out of the chapel that I wondered, was the chapel singing to me?

Chapter 14
THE
WHITE CHAPEL

When I left the Alabaster Chapel I was in a bit of a trance—the kind one only recognizes when it pops like a soap bubble some time later, returning the world to its harsher, heavier version. I was ready to leave the Open Air Museum and was passing by another masonry chapel on the way out, the White Chapel. This one is cordoned off with soft, half-inch rope strung through the tops of short metal posts positioned around the perimeter of the structure. The rope is so low it would be easy to step right over. Unlike the Alabaster Chapel whose architecture, to the layperson, might seem almost crypt-like, this square stone pavilion is raised off the ground on a tall straight foundation of sand-colored limestone. The White Chapel is covered by a solid, perfectly flat roof supported around the perimeter by twelve impressive limestone pillars—all rectangular, with sharp right angles. The slab roof's perimeter sports a cavetto cornice, a crown moulding of sorts, and under its convex arc, stripes of orange paint first applied almost 4,000 years ago still add their artistic flourish. The walls of the chapel rise from the ground and "fill in" the pillars up to about six or seven feet, resulting in 10 symmetrical rectangular windows—3 on each long side of the building, and two flanking the open doors front and rear. Standing in front of the masonry chapel, a sightline passes straight through, like a shotgun cottage in New Orleans. But these descriptions don't do it justice; they simply don't convey its irresistible geometric allure. The White Chapel is viscerally attractive.

This isn't an infatuation based on superficial beauty. Just as tempting as the handsome architecture is the fact that the White Chapel, inside and out, is decorated with what many consider the finest relief carvings in all of Egypt. I'm enchanted, basking in the warmth of the Upper Egyptian sun and what has become a daily dose of incredulity, when an Egyptian man scurries out of the proverbial woodwork. He's the first human being I've seen since entering the al fresco museum. The White Chapel is accessed via two sloping staircases, front and back, fitted with low rounded balustrades, and protected by the aforementioned string barrier, which my new acquaintance unceremoniously unclips, gesturing me to enter.

By now, I've been through quite a few temples, encountering many a "guide" offering restricted access or ancient Egyptian secrets. Are these guys modern temple guardians or clever mentalists skilled at selling exactly what spiritually starved tourists are hoping to encounter? Probably some of both, though the latter seems to be more common. It doesn't feel like these fellas even officially work at the monuments. Are they allowed to wander the temples freely, choosing their marks? Then again, they do seem to know some secrets. Remembering my experience at Dendera, I walk past an upturned palm for a private introduction to what may be the oldest building of Dynastic Egypt.

Inside are four additional rectangular pillars that I later learn were fitted with privacy veils, creating an inner sanctuary for the seated Pharaoh Senusret I. He was the first king of the Middle Kingdom, and this pavilion was erected for his Heb-Sed Festival, a traditional rite of passage held in Pharaoh's thirtieth year of rule, to demonstrate his continued virility.

The pavilion isn't the only thing erected here either. Gracing the chapel walls and columns, alongside the most delicate and detailed carvings of falcons and geese and ankhs and scarabs are images of Pharaoh Senusret receiving the blessings of the neters, especially Amun-Ra in his guise as Min, the god of procreation and fertility. Which means everywhere I look there is handsome Amun, reaching out to Senusret with an impressively long and stiff you-know-what. The proper term is ithyphallic, when one is talking about stone or statues. A side note to the sexually shy: throughout Egypt's gift shops and souvenir stands you will be confronted with keepsake carvings of the god Min, each befitted with an impossibly large penis jutting out toward potential purchasers!

I'm, uh, taking it all in, when my guide, who I've determined doesn't speak a word of English, kneels down facing a wall near the front of the chapel. Leaning forward, he places his forehead against the carved stone. At first I think he's sitting in *Salah* (religious observance) but I didn't hear the call to prayer, and I've never seen a Muslim prostrate forward to the wall.

He collects the fabric of his galabeya and maneuvers his uncooperative leather flip flops until he can stand up, then points to the wall. He's giving what are obvious instructions in a language I have only just begun to study. I shake my head.

He returns to the wall, placing his fingers upon the same carved vignette before purposefully pushing his forehead against it. Oh boy, here we go again.

When he vacates the chosen spot for a second time, I kneel down, placing my backpack on the opposite side of my body from him. With my unwieldy linen skirt forming a makeshift prayer mat, I place my forehead against the limestone wall and close my eyes.

It's lovely and cool. I bring deep breaths through my nose to my belly and back again. Then all at once, the feel of the stone against my head dissolves and in its place a scene is playing out in front of me. I see sleek boats with triangular sails slip gently against a dock, and happy people disembark. The reeds near the moorage rustle; a child has flushed some ducks who escape to the safety of the open river. Everywhere there is vivid, verdant green, and the luxurious air is heavy with the scent of flowers. The people are coming here, to Karnak Temple. I think this must have happened a long time ago. The explosion of effervescent tingles shooting through my nerves like a glass of spiritual champagne answers 'yes.'

Then like a movie being switched off, the window to that world closed.

It feels like only moments have passed, but I will never know how long I looked into that stone with my third eye. Do the temples themselves remember all they've seen? Or are there visuals stored in the stone by someone who wanted them preserved? If so, can anyone access them? Questions and doubts swirl through my mind as I place an overgenerous offering of backsheesh into a grateful foreign hand. Then I walk down the shallow stairs of the White Chapel.

Looking at my watch I find it's already a quarter to three. I don't know how long it will take me to navigate the labyrinth that is Karnak and find my way down the wide boulevard to the place where the bus is parked. I better get going.

"Shukren," I turn to wave, but the man is long gone. So it is the trees and stones who bid me godspeed as I depart the Open Air Museum just as I entered it, with only myself.

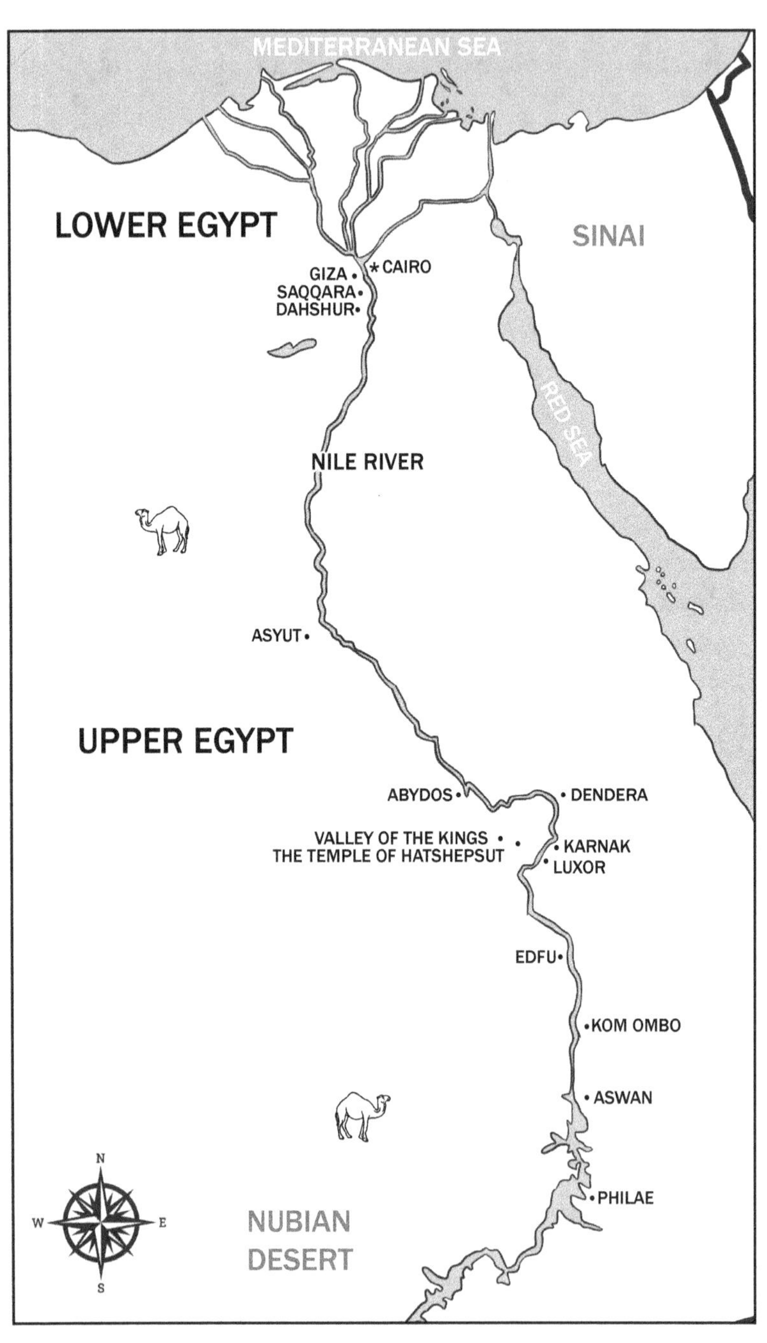

MEDITERRANEAN SEA
LOWER EGYPT
SINAI
GIZA
SAQQARA
DAHSHUR
CAIRO
RED SEA
NILE RIVER
ASYUT
UPPER EGYPT
ABYDOS
DENDERA
VALLEY OF THE KINGS
THE TEMPLE OF HATSHEPSUT
KARNAK
LUXOR
EDFU
KOM OMBO
ASWAN
PHILAE
N
W
E
S
NUBIAN
DESERT

Chapter 15

LUXOR

Ra is returning to the underworld, taking with him the last light of day. The fiery orange sun disk slowly kisses the dark waters of the Nile, the lips of Nut, captivating my eyes and soul in an ageless ritual. Twilight is gently falling and delicate brown bats are scribbling their capricious flight paths in the warm air over Luxor temple.

I'm standing back from the monument, on the wall that defines the front courtyard perimeter, looking down on the entire complex. The entry pylon, with its literally giant-sized doorway, is flanked by two nearly fifty-foot tall seated statues of Ramesses II. In front of the left colossus stands an elegant eighty-foot tall obelisk, fashioned from a single piece of pink granite. The symmetry of Luxor's entry was pillaged in 1836 when the matching twin obelisk was spirited away to the Place de la Concorde in Paris, where it stands to this day. Two additional Ramesses II stand to each side, completing the imposing front elevation. Today, the towering guards are in various states of decay. A man stands at the foot of one of the least-damaged Ramesses, preserving a memory in his camera and in my mind. I know him to be six-foot five, but he appears like a tiny toy, his shoulders no taller than the base upon which the mighty feet stand.

I've spent the last hour or so strolling the chakras of the site, rising upward like a sacred serpent through the breathtaking entry pylon, slipping through the colonnade of Amenhotep III, and finally winding my way past the grand courtyards to the temple's Holy of Holies. Is this sacred innermost chapel the third eye of the temple? Her pineal gland of sorts?

It was philosopher R.A. Schwaller de Lubicz whose 1957 treatise *Le Temple de L'Homme*, first suggested that the temple possessed divine proportions. The still-revolutionary tome reveals the results of de Lubicz's 15 years of research at Luxor. Among his sophisticated scholarship were the precise measurements of every nook and cranny (it seems) of Luxor temple. De Lubicz discovered the dimensions of the temple mapped perfectly onto the human skeleton and chakra system. He believed the temple's dimensions represented the geometry of creation itself; that it *embodied* these secrets. Could it be true what the Egyptian "Old Religion" says: the temples are a form of conscious architecture?

I'm trying to connect with the energy inside the temple but the scene is a bit frantic. Local men swirl through the dense crowd in their flowing galabeyas, trolling for tourists interested in 'secret information' and expecting to be rewarded with backsheesh.

"Are you married?" an Egyptian man asks, apparently meaning me and the Australian man walking beside me. Steve is a member of our sacred-sites tour group but our relationship is purely platonic.

"Not yet, Mate." The Aussie replies without missing a beat, confounding the temple tout who moves on to other marks.

"I'm going back to the front," I tell Steve, who nods and turns away. I watch him happily swept away by the tide of humanity.

Making my way back to Luxor's entrance was like traversing a festival crowd. In the grand court of Amenhotep III, a group of young Egyptians stopped me and asked if I would take their picture. One by one they gave me their iPhones and posed with their friends, the boys in skinny jeans and sneakers and the girls rocking hijabs and red lipstick. Together we evaluated the images on the small screens as the temple throngs flowed past. Once satisfied with the results, the twenty-somethings offered a giddy 'thank you' in English before they turned and disappeared like happy dolphins into the sea of people.

I made one last stop to gaze upon the 'walking' Ramesses II, one of the gigantic standing stone giants in Luxor known for its unique presentation. Using precise angles, and taking into account the perspective of the viewer, the anonymous ancient sculptor created a convincing illusion that this Ramesses statue is stepping forward toward the visitor.

Once out of the temple proper I make my way across the entry courtyard and back up the paved steps to the upper promenade. Here I can see the entire front pylon of Luxor temple, with it's multiple colossal Ramesses II and its remaining sky-scraping obelisk. Across the street to my right is the wide, life-giving ribbon of the Nile, choked with riverboat cruise ships. Above me, the lapis sky is closing her eyes for the night. A warm wind whips my long hair like a temple pennant.

Then all at once, the lights at the base of the temple monuments are switched on, illuminating the colonnades and architecture in all their glory. My breath catches in my throat at the sight. I'm standing alone in the darkening haze of a Luxor sunset but in my mind I'm inside the temple, walking through the Hall of Amenhotep III in a long thin dress, the scent of blue lotus on my wrists and a collar of beads on my throat, fastened by golden falcons. The temple welcomes me as I place a hand and an offering on her heart before making my way to the courtyard where the festival ceremony is taking place under the stars. The constellations have moved into place and...My memory is interrupted when a tall man I might have known here approaches and makes small talk. His voice is familiar. Over his shoulder Sirius rises. I am home.

Chapter 16

GOOD NIGHT THOTH

Egypt is a country of contrasts. It's only been about an hour since my magical sunset moment at Luxor temple and now I'm winding my way in the dark through a cacophony of car engines, tooting horns, and animated Arabic conversation, punctuated by the odd *hantour* (horse carriage) galloping by. Sara and I are navigating Mabad Al Karnak, making our way back to our hotel on the shores of the Nile. A few days ago I would have felt like I was running a psychological gauntlet, but now I know this is only an Egyptian evening. With conscious intention, I flick away small fears as they arise, and refocus on locating the intermittent sidewalks. The weather has been unusually hot, even for Egypt, and now in the cooler night air local families have emerged en masse, gathering in the park that borders the temple to visit and relax. Soon we are placing our handbags into the screening machine at the entry to our hotel, and discovering the small gift shop just beyond the checkpoint is still open.

I would like to browse but I'm getting too hungry. I have a metabolism that can go from just fine to famished in under sixty seconds. Unfortunately, Sara has developed a touch of the 'mummy's curse.' She needs to retreat to our hotel room and let the tablet Shani gave her go to work on her tummy troubles. Katie, another woman in the group, has just passed the checkpoint. I like her a lot and am hoping a friendship might develop.

"Hi Katie."

"Hi."

"I'm going to the hotel bar to have a bite to eat and a glass of champagne. Have you seen it? It's really something. Would you like to join me?"

Our group is staying at an elegant historic hotel. There are two pools and a new modern building where our accommodations are located, but the original grand lobby, formal sitting room, and ritzy bar have a refined Victorian décor that probably hasn't changed since Howard Carter's time!

"Sure, I need to go to my room first."

I nod but the day's adrenaline has suddenly and without warning metabolized into a crushing fatigue. I'm afraid if I stop off at our hotel room and sit down I'll lose my motivation to socialize. If I were to lean back on the bed, it would be room service for sure. This is our last night at the hotel, so it's my final chance to have a drink at the swanky bar. A quick glance downward reveals my skirt and top seem fine, if a bit seasoned. Nothing a spritz of perfume won't fix.

"OK, I'm heading over there now," I reply. I am not going to consider not going. I probably just need to eat something.

"I'll meet you there in a few minutes," Katie veers left down the garden path that leads to the property's newer wing.

I keep straight and then climb the stairs to the traditional hotel. The wide carpeted hallway in the main building is eerily empty. I peek over a red velvet rope into an open ballroom which turns out to be the formal dining room. A sign hangs on the podium near the door: Reservations Required. It's closed anyway. I guess these days most guests prefer the al fresco poolside cafe with live music and shisha, the Egyptian tobacco smoked from free standing brass hookahs.

After slipping into a ladies room and brushing my Luxor-wrecked hair, I float into the dimly lit wood-paneled bar and find an open corner. The bench seats are low and luxurious, with velvet-encased down pillows reclining against the wall. The cocktail table is dressed with votive candles and a glass ashtray holding a slim box of matches. To the side, a slim black leather folder contains the menu. To my delight it includes splits of champagne and beef sliders.

Katie arrives and it doesn't take long before two flutes of champagne are placed before us on the low table. We talk about our families and how we came to be on the trip. In addition to all things Egyptian, we are both interested in the Anunnaki of ancient Sumer, especially the goddesses and their legends of long-life, even immortality. We agree their similarities to the Egyptian pantheon are intriguing.

The sliders arrive, which rank among the best I've enjoyed anywhere. I didn't realize how hungry I was. In between bites Katie and I carefully divulge a few psychic and spiritual events that have changed us, along with some hopes for the future. I'm relieved to discover Katie seems intelligent, grounded, and doesn't take herself too seriously. In the past I've explored friendships with 'spiritual' people only to find the conversation careening off into what I can only describe as delusion. One cup of ayahuasca slurped does not a shaman make. I'm a Taoist at heart and in my experience the person who tells me how enlightened they are becoming is probably not becoming enlightened. I can spot a true master a mile away. He or she is the one who can't stop laughing.

Soon Katie and I are giggling, arm in arm, as we make our way across the manicured lawn back toward our rooms in the newer wing. Night insects sing along with the *darbukas* (Egyptian hand drums) from the live band as we weave our way between the trees trying to find the path. In the end we discover our rooms are not as close as we thought and say farewell. Soft night air wraps me like a warm towel as I walk back to my room escorted by Thoth, the moon god of wisdom. Sara is asleep in her bed but manages to tell me she's feeling better. I want to share about the evening but she's instantly unconscious again.

Crawling into my bed by the window, the last thing I remember is Thoth's silvery light through the sheer privacy curtains.

That night I dream of temple Priests wearing leopard skins and black eyeliner. I walk though clouds of burning incense and recognize the fragrances of frankincense and myrrh. I hear the sounds we use to call the gods, to awaken the temples. I am told I won't remember them, but I know I will. Forever.

"Callan, wake up. I have some coffee for you." Sara is holding a steaming mug near my nose.

"Thank you," I take the cup groggily, propping myself up with my bed pillows.

"What were you dreaming about?"

I'm staring through the filmy drapes at the orange flowers climbing over the low stucco wall of our ground floor patio room, trying to mentally grip the dream as it slips away. A few images remain but they're more like visual feelings; not anything I can describe with words. I take a sip of strong black coffee.

"I was waking the temples."

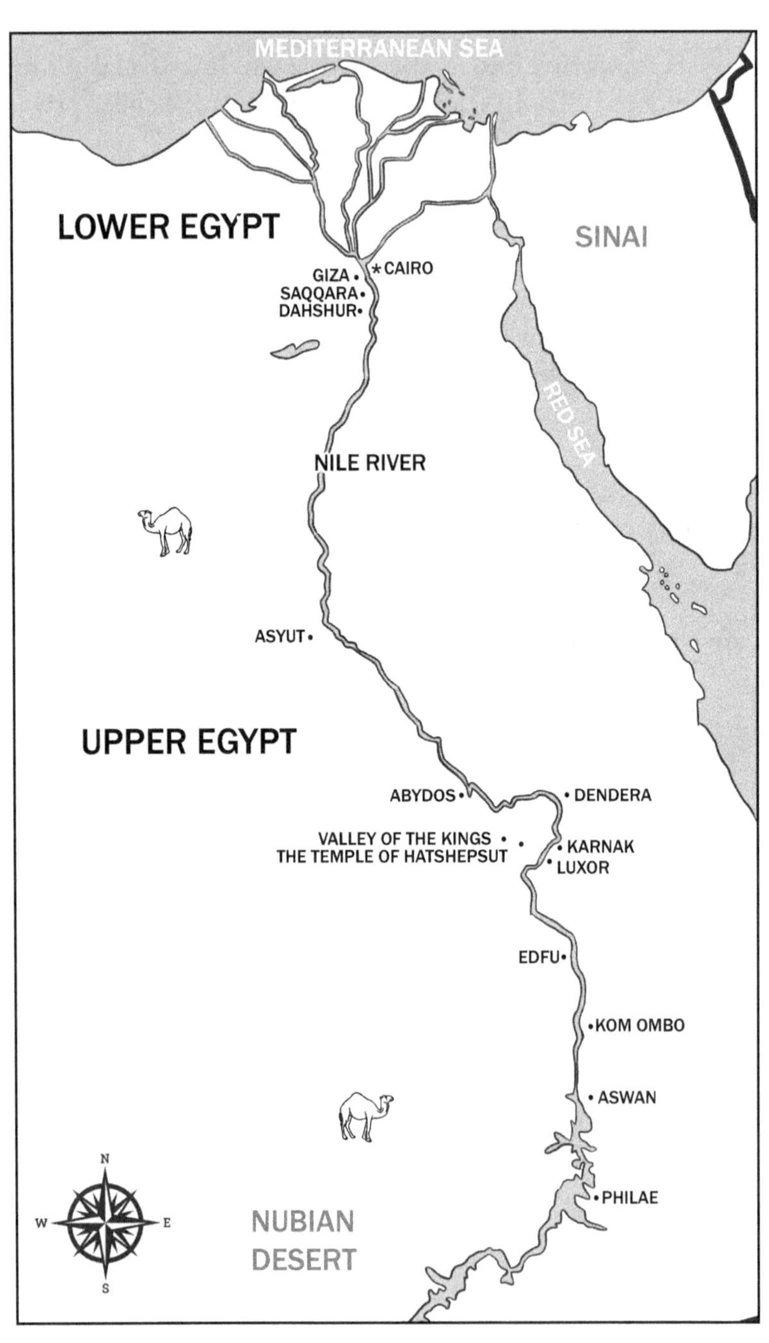

MEDITERRANEAN SEA
LOWER EGYPT
SINAI
GIZA
SAQQARA
DAHSHUR
CAIRO
RED SEA
NILE RIVER
ASYUT
UPPER EGYPT
ABYDOS
DENDERA
VALLEY OF THE KINGS
THE TEMPLE OF HATSHEPSUT
KARNAK
LUXOR
EDFU
KOM OMBO
ASWAN
PHILAE
N
W
E
S
NUBIAN
DESERT

Chapter 17

THE TEMPLE OF HATSHEPSUT

From Luxor, one must travel west across the Nile to reach Deir al Bahri and the temple of Queen Hatshepsut. The vast car park, where all the jumbo tour buses are stabled side by side is virtually empty. Nonetheless, I make a mental note to memorize the exterior features of our vehicle as I exit. At the Giza plateau I learned that by afternoon, the buses at the monuments can multiply exponentially. That afternoon at the pyramids, I wandered through a strange village of rainbow colored coaches, indentured camels, and cigarette smoking bus drivers until I eventually recognized our security man standing near the open door of the correct vehicle.

I still haven't quite gotten used to it, always having an armed bodyguard sitting in the very first passenger seat of the bus, positioned directly behind the driver for optimum defensive advantage. The Egyptian government is deadly serious about keeping tourists safe. In 1997, sixty-two tourists were murdered by terrorists right here in Deir el Bahri. Though terrorist attacks have decreased greatly, only six months ago a tour bus just like ours was bombed at the Giza Pyramids. I choose to avoid conditioning my quantum field with thoughts like that, so instead, I notice today's detail has a starched, button-down brown shirt with short sleeves, revealing naturally well-muscled arms and an intimidating, military-style timepiece. And of course, there's the gun on his hip. I know he'll wait patiently for the last passenger to file by and disembark the bus before he discretely joins us, tracking us so expertly that we often forget he's nearby.

Stepping down the steep, narrow bus stairs is as awkward as it was in grade school and today the last sideways jump-step to the ground is truly un–elegant for a petite woman in a long, slim cotton dress. I've come to expect and appreciate the one or two chivalrous Egyptian men who often make the de–busing more pleasant.

Like most days, the transition from the air-conditioned motor coach to heat–softened asphalt is like walking into a sauna fully clothed. I'm unable to read the Arabic writing branding the glaring metal flank of our vehicle so I commit to memory the bright orange graphic and tangerine colored curtains that have been drawn to keep the interior cool while we're gone.

And then we walk. Up and around a primitive, sweltering road and into a wide, sheltered breezeway lined with tourist shops. Cotton dresses and shirts embroidered with Egyptian motifs are hung everywhere, dancing tirelessly to the ceaseless breath of the oversized ceiling fans humming within their metal cages. The garments must fight for attention amidst tables overflowing with carved gods and goddesses and Egyptian costume jewelry that most likely did not originate in Egypt. Here's a tip I learned from the proprietor of an upscale souvenir shop in Luxor: If you hold a lighter's flame to a stone statuette, and it starts to melt, you are being hoodwinked into buying a cheap resin knock-off. A limestone, basalt, or granite carving will obviously not soften in response to heat. I'm not sure how many vendors would allow a customer to burn the merchandise before buying, but anyway, now you know.

By now I know better than to pause, or look too interested in the wares for fear of being uncomfortably trailed by desperate shopkeepers, who I know are only just trying to feed their families. But then I catch sight of a shapely, headless black mannequin wearing a stretchy black and gold striped Beladi-style dress, fringed with gold coins!

Beladi (which translates literally as country or rural) lends its name to an authentic style of Egyptian folk dance: Raqs Beladi, or dance of the country. Beladi is also the vernacular for a hugely popular middle eastern drum beat properly known as Small Masmoudi. I teach Egyptian dance back in the USA and I've been looking for something to wear to our cruise ship's on-board Egyptian dance night. This one has the traditional longer sleeves, slit up to the elbows, that I convince myself will compensate, respectability-wise, for its low plunging neckline held precariously together by thin straps of shiny gold sequins. I own a gold, crystal-encrusted performance bra—the stiff kind that stands up on its own—

which would be perfect underneath, but I didn't dare pack it after reading the clothing recommendations for visiting a Muslim country. Then I remember a nude-colored tank top in my suitcase which could provide the required modesty layer.

The thirty-something proprietor senses my interest immediately and begins to undress the mannequin, waving me in. Once removed from the plastic figure, it's obvious the dress is way too big and had been pinned for display. The tag says M/L.

"Too big," I say, then regret speaking to him like a toddler when he replies.

"It's too big for you miss, of course, I'll go get you your size. What size?"

"I need a size small, but we're on our way to the temple." I suddenly feel like an insect who has flown too close to a spider's web, moments away from being totally ensnared. "I'm sorry, I have to go now."

He's following me down the breezeway.

"I'll get you small dress. Small. Please come back, Okay?" he pleads, smiling, before breaking off the chase like a lioness who has let too much space come between her paws and her prey.

"Okay," I call back, feeling like I've promised too much.

The last shop in the breezeway is selling chilled Nescafe, which I purchase without incident. It's an old fashioned beer-style cap, not screw top, which the boy pops off gratis. I slip the young kid a few extra pounds, just because. Holding the cold bottle to my cheek like a lover, I notice the storefronts have successfully snagged a good number of people from our bus. No one seems in any hurry and I find myself second-guessing my decision to flee the belly dance dress. Eventually, the entire group moves through the shaded retail tunnel to emerge into the shopping afterlife, brilliant and blinding from Ra's satisfied smile. The last thing one passes by on the gravelly road before approaching the entrance to the temple proper is a limestone block building with a large painted sign that says, in both Arabic and English: Hatshepsut Ambulance.

Emerging onto the wide avenue and seeing Hatshepsut's temple for the first time is surreal. The first shock is the height of the rock cliffs that rise behind the structure. How did I not see these cliffs before? They remind me of Sedona, Arizona's red rock mesas except bland. By bland I mean there's no color anywhere for as far as the eye can see. Or rather there's only one color: a yellow-beige sand. The bricks paving the wide avenue of approach are this color, the ground is this color, the temple is this color, and the cliffs are this color. It's as if everything's been unsaturated in Photoshop, except the cerulean sky. And my dress, which is red. I'm thinking about my dress because at this moment, darker accents are highlighting my female anatomy on the fabric like a red shroud of Turin. It is so hot that my thin cotton dress is starting to soak through with perspiration. Above 112 degrees Fahrenheit, even natural fabrics are no match for the Egyptian sun.

A fickle breeze provides the opportunity to unstick the dress from my belly, and, after Sara takes some photos of me standing in front of the temple, we walk to Queen Hatshepsut's legacy.

The wide avenue of approach extends over 300 feet to the first staircase, after which low stone balustrades line the gently ascending series of ramps, ensuring the complete visual vulnerability of arriving visitors. The brazen authority of the architecture, all right angles and imposing columns is visually intimidating, likely designed to be so—a fitting architectural representation of a female Pharaoh boldly asserting her god-given right to rule.

Hatshepsut was a New Kingdom Pharaoh who ruled for twenty years in the middle of the Eighteenth Dynasty (roughly 1,300-1,550 BCE). She took the throne after her husband, Pharaoh Thutmose II, passed, establishing herself as Pharaoh despite the customs of the times. Her reign was a Renaissance of sorts, when Egyptian commerce and art once again flourished after the country was reclaimed from the Hyskos kings of the Sixteenth and Seventeenth Dynasties. Although the majestic statues lining the mezzanine at Deir El Bahri depict her as a male wearing the false pharaonic beard, there is no evidence to indicate she dressed as a man in real life. It was only after her stepson, Thutmose III, took the throne that many of her likenesses were transitioned and her accomplishments marginalized.

In the Arab tradition, the historian Mas Udi tells us that an unnamed woman Pharaoh, a sorceress, protected Egypt by magical spells for the thirty years following the Exodus; that walls she built around the borders of Egypt held magical statues of crocodiles, lions, and other fierce creatures she could summon to life. She collected many magical papyri, learned the properties of plants, animals, and minerals, and controlled the powers of nature. By burying magical wax men in the ground, she caused the enemies of Egypt to be swallowed up by the Earth. The pharaonic sorceress must have been none other than Hatshepsut.[24]

Hatshepsut appears to have been steeped in the Old Religion. She created elaborately decorated chapels to honor the goddess Hathor and the god Anubis within the iconic hillside temple she built. Anubis is well known in popular culture, traditionally depicted as a man with the head of a black dog or jackal. He is the Opener of The Way, the lord of the dead who guards the deceased and prepares the body for the afterlife. In the Duat, Anubis accompanies the dead to the Halls of Osiris for the weighing of the heart ceremony. In this ritual, the heart of the deceased is placed on one side of a scale. A single feather from the headdress of Ma'at, Goddess of Truth, is placed on the other side. If the heart is as light as a feather, the soul is granted immortality, for it was the heart that remembered all the deeds of life.[25] If the heart was heavier than the feather, the soul was tossed into the gaping maw of a waiting monster crocodile known as Ammit.

Incidentally, though Anubis is far more famous, another jackal-headed god, called Anpu or Wepawet is also known as Opener of the Way. Like Anubis, Wepawet is a beneficent and loyal guardian. Whereas Anubis is opener of the roads to the north and personifies the summer solstice,

---

[24]Houston, Jean. 1995. *The Passion of Isis and Osiris.* Ballantine/Wellspring (Random House), NY, p. 169.

[25]Houston, Jean. 1995. *The Passion of Isis and Osiris.* Ballantine/Wellspring (Random House), NY, p. 351.

Wepawet is opener of the roads to the south and personifies the winter solstice.[26]

On the far side of Hatshepsut's temple, opposite the area dedicated to Anubis, is the temple of Hathor, the beloved Egyptian goddess of sexual love, dance, music, drinking, and childbirth. On each side of the stone doorway leading to the sanctuary, slim orange staff-like columns topped with painted Hathor heads are remarkably well preserved for being painted thousands of years ago! Hathor's trademark halo of hair (presumed to be a wig) is painted vivid turquoise. Once inside I am again dwarfed by sandstone columns, each adorned with a carved visage of the goddess. The wide, almost triangular faces feature aristocratic noses, oversized eyes, full lips and wide cheekbones that slope dramatically inward to the chin. She's beautiful, but not like anyone I've ever seen. She's not quite human. On each carving, Hathor's small cow ears are visible in front of her hair. When not portrayed as a woman with cow-like ears, Hathor is often shown as a lithe goddess wearing her signature headdress: a sun disk uplifted by two cow horns. At other times Hathor appears completely cow-like.

"All Pharaohs, by virtue of the title, were considered children of Hathor," reminds Shani, pointing to the wall behind me. "She is often seen nursing important people."

Turning to look, my eyes rise up the sandstone wall of this temple–within–a–temple. There, high above me, I see an enormous, exquisite carving of a beautiful female bovine. Below her belly is the suckling pharaoh. Hung around the

---

[26]Houston, Jean. 1995. *The Passion of Isis and Osiris.* Ballantine/ Wellspring (Random House), NY, p. 169.

animal's neck where one would expect to see a cowbell dangles an elegant ankh, the symbol of eternal life.

Hathor may be the nurturing mother of humanity, a sacred cow goddess, but she is also the goddess of sexual love. Some people believe the art of sexual alchemy was taught here at Deir el Bahri, perhaps in this very temple.

Or possibly the temple next door.

Immediately adjacent to Hatshepsut's terraced temple lies the Temple of Mentuhotep. There, archaeologists have discovered graves of "Priestesses of Hathor."[27] Hatshepsut herself may have been a Priestess in the cult of Isis, which taught sacred sexuality as a form of spiritual alchemy into Greek times.

Perhaps it was Hatshepsut's expedition to the land of Punt, which she documented on her temple walls, that inspired her interest in Hathor, or perhaps it was the other way around. Hathor is said to have come from Punt in predynastic (or possibly prehistoric) times. This "mythical" land "to the east" of Egypt may have been on the southern shores of the Red Sea, the Sinai Peninsula, or even farther east in ancient Sumer. The fact that Hatshepsut documented the expedition and brought back exotic luxuries—including Myrrh trees that she planted in her Egyptian temple—seem to indicate Punt was a real destination.

This is intriguing because Hathor and the Sumerian goddess Ninmah may be one and the same. Speaking of

---

[27]Wikipedia. *Deir el-Bahari Mortuary temple of Nebhepetre Mentuhotep (https://en.wikipedia.org/wiki/Deir_el-Bahari).* Accessed on August 19, 2022.

Hathor, author Tricia McCannon explains, "It is from her original Sumerian name Ninmah that we get the word Ma or Mama today. As the chief medical officer of the Anunnaki gods, she was assigned to earth. Ninmah is one of the three gods responsible for the genetic engineering of humankind."[28]

Hathor and Anubis weren't the only ancient neters that Hatshepsut venerated. She was a devotee of the primordial god Amun and repaired a good portion of his temple in Thebes (modern day Luxor) during her reign. It was Hatshepsut who erected those two obelisks near the entrance to Karnak temple. The one I saw a few days ago is the tallest ancient obelisk on earth! Later, Queen Hatshepsut added two additional obelisks at Karnak to celebrate her sixteenth year as Pharaoh. Under Hatshepsut's care, order and abundance were restored along the Nile. Prosperity flowed.

Hatshepsut, with her round cheeks and large eyes, may have ruled the last peaceful period in Egypt, the early Eighteenth Dynasty. In the latter half of the Eighteenth Dynasty, Amenhotep III passed the pharaonic torch to his son Amenhotep IV, later known as Akhenaten. Akhenaten was strange and beautiful; both he and his famously lovely wife Nefertiti are carved in busts with extremely elongated skulls. Akhenaten's father and mother, Amenhotep III and Tiye have the tragic distinction of being the last rulers of a spiritually aligned Egypt. By the time Akhenaten took the throne, perfidious Egyptian priests worshipped a new pantheon of money, power, and misogyny.

---

[28]McCannon, Tricia. 2015. *The Return of the Divine Sophia*. Bear & Company, VT, p. 458.

Akhenaten was apparently a lover, not a fighter, for he simply walked away from the temples—and the capital of Egypt—to establish a new monotheistic way of worship and a new, uncorrupted capital city, Tel El Amarna. Here, a single deity was honored, represented in artwork as a round sun disk from which rays of immortalizing energy radiated. Akhenaten called it the Aten. To what degree Akhenaten's bold actions were in response to the malfeasance of the temple priests or his unwavering devotion to his new god, the Aten, is unclear. What is known is that the beginning of the end of Egypt's Old Religion had begun. Even when Akhenaten's son, King Tutankhamen, abandoned his father's dogma and reverted to ruling in conventional fashion, the boy's reign was short-lived. Physically and politically weak, the now-famous king succumbed to a suspicious death at age nineteen. The royal bloodline died with him.

That is a lot of history to unpack. I'm walking with Sara past Hatshepsut Ambulance, retracing our steps back to the bus. As we enter the shopping breezeway, the merchant with the belly dance dress pounces.

"Here is a small dress!" he beams and hands me a striped gold garment packaged inside a clear plastic pouch.

We stop and I unseal the sleeve, extracting the dress to examine it. It is the same style dress. When I check, the tag says "S." Holding it up to myself, it actually seems like it will fit!

Confident the sale is made, the shopkeeper strides away, leaving me holding the dress. He clearly has this dialed in. I have, in fact, decided to buy the dress. When we approach his stall, the gentleman produces two small, chilled glasses of hibiscus tea, handing one to each of us.

"Shukren," I sit down in the metal folding chair he has ceremoniously wedged between stacks of t-shirts and tables piled high with unidentified items enshrined in cellophane like my dress. It's still hot as hell but a fan in the corner of the retail booth offers intermittent absolution. Evidently there is only one chair so Sara is forced to sit on the cement step with her tea. As always, her mood remains pleasant. Sara's ability to happily adapt makes her a stressless travel companion and a truly precious friend. Soon the negotiations start and the drama seems way out of proportion to the little dress. This isn't a professional cabaret costume by a Cairo designer, just a thin little beladi dress made for tourists.

Looking around I notice the other merchants eyeing us and realize no other shoppers have taken a seat anywhere. Our shopkeeper Mohamed (I have discovered his name) is grinning like a Cheshire cat and I sense his capture of us is a real coup among the street vendors. I try out a few Egyptian phrases on him which I discover work like the ancient magic on the surprised shopkeepers. Between unpredictable eruptions of good-natured laughter, Mohamed corrects my pronunciation as best he can and we return to finalizing the finances for the dress. I'm beginning to get it. The bartering is part of the fun for these guys. It's a bit of a game.

Since I really do have to watch my spending money, I decide to embrace the barter. Pulling out some tricks I learned in Bali, I propose a fair price for the dress. Mohamed feigns insult, then counteroffers. Back and forth we dance until I make my final offer. To have us get up and leave without consummating the sale would surely be an embarrassment, not to mention the lost return on his time investment. Mohamed accepts. Then the shrewd salesman suggests adding items to the sale. But I'm done.

"*Kallas*" I reply sweetly. In Egyptian Arabic it means "finished."

"Bravo!" he replies, approving of my word choice and pronunciation.

I place the notes in his hand, "Shukren, Mohamed."

"Afwan, Callan."

"Did you find a dance costume?" Michael asks as I settle into my bus seat near the window. In the aisle, Sara is stowing and re-stowing her bags in the overhead shelf with the focus of a dog making its bed in a blanket.

"Yes, I did!"

"Wonderful," he replies, holding my gaze for a little too long.

Chapter 18

THE VALLEY OF THE KINGS

Egypt's Valley of the Kings is probably the country's third most famous site after the Giza Pyramids and the Sphinx. It was here in 1922 that archaeologist Howard Carter and his team unearthed modern history's richest cache of relics, including the undisturbed mummy of King Tutankhamen. The golden-masked mummy, along with his elaborate burial treasures, bestowed wealth, fame and some believe, untimely death on its twentieth-century defilers.

Incidentally, it was an Egyptian water boy working

on the dig, not Howard Carter himself, who initially discovered the signs of the underground shaft that led into Tutankhamen's tomb. It's a sad comment on turn-of-the-century British colonialism that history doesn't even mention the lad's name.

The Valley of the Kings is today's famous destination. A winding, featureless road wraps the rocky foothills leading up to the valley, which our ecologically unfit tourist coach is laboriously climbing. When we finally get to the car park, it is empty except for several police cars parked headlight to headlight across the huge cement squares. Has something happened? As we get out, I notice our driver conferring with the Egyptian cops but I can't hear what they're saying.

No time to find out for a small train of sorts has arrived—the kind with multiple open air 'cars' fitted with bench seats and canopies, and pulled by an ATV-like vehicle. It's something one might see at a zoo or at Disneyland to take visitors from the hinterlands of the car park to the entry gate. We are each given a water bottle and climb into a seat for the lift to the top of the hill. Despite a protective coating of SPF 30 I feel a hot sizzle on my arm as we jerk into motion. Scooting inward toward the shaded center of the bench, I watch the pavement slide slowly past. I think I could walk to the top as fast as this thing's going! Instead, I lean back and relax, letting the mechanical caterpillar inch me closer and closer to the tombs of the Pharaohs. Eventually the tram slides to a squeaky stop and I step out into the Valley of the Kings.

And what a valley it is! The valley's flanks rise upward, as desiccated and dry as an Egyptian mummy's thighs. There is no vegetation at all, only rocks strewn across the sandy rolling hills. I uncap my water bottle, noticing it's nearly empty already! The wet liquid is heavenly on my cracked lips, but they dry instantly after each sip. I recap my bottle and push it into the side pocket of my leather backpack before threading my arm through the straps. Then, as if in a dream, my shoes crunch up the gravel to the tomb entrances of the Valley of the Kings. The violent gashes carved into the foothills by Egyptologists and tomb robbers are now dressed with tidy masonry walls that lead down to locked metal doors. These are the entrances to the Pharaohs' tombs. Shani is giving us an orientation.

This Pharaoh was buried here and such and such a Pharaoh is up the hill on the right and I have stopped walking, overtaken with the eerie silence of this place. I have been wondering if I would feel the spirits of the many people interred here, but they have long since gone.

"Concealed all over this mountain are 62 known tombs that once hid the meticulously prepared bodies of the Egyptian nobility," Shani continues.

Michael notices me staring up at the pyramid-shaped mountain looming over the necropolis. Wispy, translucent clouds cling to its faraway peak.

"The Pharaohs had themselves buried here because that is the sacred mountain," he explains, "Dehenet-Imentet, one of the primordial mounds that the gods consecrated at Zep Tepi. The Egyptians believed a sacred goddess lived in the mountain, that she was the mountain."

"Hmmm," The desolate canyon and barren mountain seem very un-goddess-like to me. Dry, silent, and still, but not in a dark way. In an immortal way.

Later I discovered that Dehenet-Imentet also means "Peak of the West," and that it was the goddess Hathor (known as "Lady of the Peak") who was believed to dwell in the mountain and in some sense was the mountain. The site is also linked to Meretseger, a goddess whose name means, "She Who Loves Silence," an appropriate name for a goddess whose domain was mostly inhabited by the dead and a small village of craftsmen and their families.[29]

Shani has assembled the group in front of the entrance to KV11, the tomb of Ramses III.

"I am not allowed to come with you into the tomb," she explains. "Tourist guides are not permitted in any of the tombs out of respect for the dead who are buried here. The guard will punch your ticket as you enter. Silence is required in the tombs at all times. You can take pictures with your phones, but do not take out a camera unless you have already purchased a photo pass."

Shani leads us toward two angular masonry walls that border a roofless path downward. At the end, another caramel-colored rock wall holds a tall locking gate fashioned of steel bars. For added security, thick wire mesh—now rusted the color of dried blood—lines the inside of the barred portal. Beyond there is only darkness; a literal gateway to the underworld. I wonder how many feet I will have to stoop or crawl to reach the Pharaoh's burial chamber.

---

[29] Association for the Study of Women and Mythology. *Tales of the Two Lands (womenandmyth.org)*. Accessed on August 19, 2022.

"Remember, this is a very sacred site," she implores as we file past.

It's hard to say if Shani is more concerned with her charges getting into trouble with the monument authorities or incurring a more supernatural consequence. Many people still believe it was the "curse of the mummy" from the tomb just up the hill that caused a multitude of tragedies to befall Howard Carter and others involved with the King Tut excavation.

I hand my ticket to the entry guard without saying a word and step into the entry shaft of Ramesses III's final resting place. Sturdy wide wooden steps lead down and *Oh My God!*

I'm standing upright on a varnished, wooden plank walkway which slopes gently down into a tall, spacious rock-cut tunnel. Warm lighting installed along the floor bathes the walls in a golden glow, revealing scene after colorful scene of exquisitely carved and painted gods, winged goddesses, slithering sentient snakes, ankhs, cartouches, and hieroglyphs. It feels more like an art gallery than a tomb. Everywhere there are brightly painted hieroglyphs! The ceiling is covered wall-to-wall with a perfect pattern of small five pointed stars on an inky background. Down the center of the ceiling, a vivid yellow ribbon bisects the stone firmament, filled with mysterious hieroglyphs. This is the Litany of Ra, which is often found near the entrances to tombs.

The Litany of Ra is a New Kingdom funerary text that invokes the sun god Ra in his seventy-five forms. Then it proceeds to a spell which assists the discarnate pharaoh in assuming the elements of nature and the various neters, finally culminating in a transcendental reunion between the deceased spirit and the solar deity himself.

Walking deeper into the mountain, I notice some of the ubiquitous artwork is reminiscent of the carvings on the walls of Dendera and other Dynastic temples. Yet here, in the Valley of the Kings, one can see the masonry canvases as the artists intended, undamaged by the blowing sands of time and the smothering smoke of Bedouin fires. But the vivid colors of the tomb's artwork are slowly fading. Although a modern glass barrier has been erected to keep sweaty hands off the sacred scenes, the clear panels do nothing to shield the ancient pigments from the exhalations of visitors. Sadly, increased humidity and carbon dioxide from breathing humans is slowly degrading the tombs' technicolor décor. You see, these magical illustrations were never meant for living eyes to see. They were left here for the soul of the deceased pharaoh. They are a guidebook to the underworld.

I'm nearing the end of Ramesses III's 410 foot long tomb (which seems an excessive distance to carry a corpse) but this isn't the longest shaft in the Valley of the Kings. The longest tomb actually belongs to a Queen. Queen Hatshepsut's burial chamber is nearly 700 feet from the entrance and descends 320 feet (100 meters) into the rock.[30]

Now I'm hundreds of feet in and it's become obvious there is absolutely no ventilation. The lower you go, the muggier it becomes. But I can't turn back now. I want to see the depiction of another famous Egyptian funerary text in a

---

[30]Drower, Margaret Stefana. *Valley of the Kings*. Encyclopedia Britannica, *(https://www.britannica.com/place/Valley-of-the-Kings)*. Accessed on August 19, 2022.

corridor near the burial chamber. I want to see with my own eyes what is in the underworld. Literally, that's the name of the text. The Amduat, (translation: *The Book of What is in the Duat*) depicts the twelve hours of the night the barque (boat) of Ra must journey, traversing the underworld before rising again.

The Egyptians believed that the soul (Ba) of the deceased made this same mystical journey, fraught with danger and promise, before arriving in the Halls of Osiris.

The twelve regions/hours of the Duat are:

Hour 1: The sun god enters the western horizon (akhet) which is a transition between day and night.

Hours 2 and 3: He passes through an abundant watery world called 'Wernes' and the 'Waters of Osiris'.

Hour 4: He reaches Imhet, the difficult sandy realm of Seker the underworld hawk deity, where he encounters dark zig zag pathways which he must negotiate, being dragged on a snake-boat.

Hour 5: He discovers the tomb of Osiris which is an enclosure beneath which is hidden a lake of fire. The tomb is covered by a pyramid-like mound (identified with the goddess Isis) on top of which Isis and Nephthys have alighted in the form of two kites (birds of prey).

Hour 6: The most significant event in the underworld occurs. The ba (soul) of Ra unites with his own body, or alternatively with the ba of Osiris within the circle formed by the mehen serpent. This event is the point at which the sun begins its regeneration; it is a moment of great significance, but also danger.

Hour 7: The adversary Apep (Apophis) lies in wait and has to be subdued in chains by the magic of Isis and Ser, and the strength of Serqet, who is assisted by the god Her-Tesu-F.

Hour 8: The sun god opens the doors of the tomb and Horus calls upon a monstrous serpent with the unquenchable fire to destroy the enemies of his father, Osiris, by burning their corpses and cooking their souls.

Hour 9: They leave the sandy island of Seker by rowing vigorously back into the waters.

Hour 10: The regeneration process continues through immersion in the waters.

Hour 11: The god's eyes (a symbol for his health and well being) are fully regenerated.

Hour 12: He enters the eastern horizon ready to rise again as the new day's sun.

Once the deceased finished their journey through the underworld, they arrived at the Hall of Ma'at. Here they would undergo the Weighing of the Heart ceremony. The petitioners' purity would determine whether they would be allowed to enter the Kingdom of Osiris, and the heart was both judge and jury.

For the well-prepared, there were a few work-arounds. The ritual of placing a gemstone scarab on the physical heart of a mummy, for example, was neither purely decorative nor symbolic. The heart was the only organ not removed during mummification. During the Weighing of the Heart ceremony it was hoped the enchanted scarab would appeal to the heart not to speak against the soul, ensuring a successful transition to the underworld.

When I ascend from the underworld beneath Dehenet, Ra is high in the sky. The frail cirrus clouds tickling the top of the mountain have long since burned away. I decide to take a break in the covered visitor's rest area but by the time I get there I am a literal hot mess. Attempting to wipe makeup from under one eye and then the other, my finger slips along my skin like an out-of-control ice skater. The ceiling fans are spinning but in the open air pavilion there is only oven-hot air to circulate. A couple other ladies have joined me and flip open paper accordion fans they have stashed in their bags. Soon the copy-cats, myself and Sara included, have repurposed papers and maps and whatever we can find into makeshift handheld fans. Back and forth we flutter like a group of hothouse butterflies alighted on a bush.

From the elevated perch of the outdoor traveler's sanctuary (and I use that word lightly) I watch people emerge from the tombs, wiping their brows and looking around. We have had the Valley of the Kings almost to ourselves this morning, but just a few years ago, up to 5,000 people a day walked up and down these tombs. No wonder the paint in the tombs is panting for life.

The wobbly train ride back down to the car park is even stickier after a morning in the sweltering tombs but the effort was well worth it. Bumping along, I realize the previously vague distinction between Egyptian tomb shafts and pyramid shafts is no longer confusing me. Authors like John Anthony West have described the dramatic differences, but experiencing them in person drives the points home. Though they both feature rectangular shafts sloping down for hundreds of feet through solid stone, the completely undecorated pyramid shafts are cramped, very narrow, and not tall enough for anyone but a small child to stand upright in.

The glorious tombs, on the other hand, feel almost like strolling a subterranean museum hall, where plumb straight walls and massive columns display endless works of fine ancient art. I have to remind myself the sophisticated symbolism, stylish figures, and bold colors were meant for only one purpose: to assist the Pharaoh in his or her afterlife. Once the tombs were sealed, the meticulous masterpieces covering just about every surface from floor to ceiling (including the ceiling!) would never be seen again. Or at least that's what they thought before the tomb robbers, archaeologists, and the occasional unfortunate need to reuse a burial chamber made the sanctity of the mummy moot.

We're mid-way down the Valley of the Kings, transferring from the mini-train to our tourist bus for the final portion of the descent when I realize what has happened. Katie's small form is crumpled across the very first bus seat. Her forehead is furrowed in pain and small kitten sounds are squeaking from her throat. She's crying. Crying like someone who doesn't want to use her lungs.

"What happened!?"

"Katie fell off the train," explains a young man in the group.

Fell off the train? He can't possibly be talking about the slow-moving tram.

The tour leaders and a doctor in the group are needing space to tend to Katie, so we mill around outside the open door of the bus.

I'm really concerned. First, it seems like you'd have to work really hard to get yourself flung off the mild-mannered little "train." Second, Katie is super cool and youthful, but she's also a skinny white grandmother. Just the type of woman the television commercials are always pleading with to take meds for osteoporosis.

"How did she fall off?" I ask the closest person, who happens to be another woman on the tour, Ebony.

"The train was turning one way and Katie was leaning the other way and she just rolled out the open side and onto the ground." Ebony was with her when it happened. She seems as surprised as I do.

Finally, we are allowed to board the bus. Sobered from the shock, we walk silently down the central metal plank of the vehicle and solemnly take our seats. I don't remember looking out the windows—all I remember is arriving at the ship dock where we would board the much anticipated 4-night Nile cruise without Katie.

I never did have the opportunity to cultivate the easy rapport between Katie and I into a friendship. She left for a Cairo hospital that night where she would be treated for broken ribs and a shattered ankle. Although we were able to send a group card and flowers, only a few days later she was medevaced in a 747 back to the States. When Michael broke the news to the group, he said Katie was in good spirits and had committed to completing the trip at some point in the future. I really hope she will.

Chapter 19

SAILING THE NILE

A cruise down the Nile River is as romantic as it sounds, except when your cabin mate is your best friend and there is literally one foot of space between the two twin beds filling your tiny cabin. But nothing could irritate me right now! We have boarded a riverboat a la *Death on the Nile*, and are sailing from Luxor in Upper Egypt toward the even more exotic Nubian desert region which straddles the Egyptian-Sudanese border. I slide the glass door to our miniature balcony open and despite the instant spike in humidity and the faint smell of diesel, the scenery is luxurious. For someone like myself who lives in a juniper and sagebrush desert, the shore flowing slowly past with its impossibly dense reeds, emerald green foliage, and the occasional stately date palm is positively decadent. The blue water and occasional flying bird soothe my soul, reminding me of the coastal town I grew up in. Beyond the riverbanks, farmed fields stretch away in fertile rows of brown and green, punctuated by linen-colored donkeys with grey points and the round rumps of plentiful fodder. Without the sound of farm machinery, the agriculture feels peaceful, unhurried, nonviolent. Where the wetlands reach out farther toward the open river, several cows and a bull are grazing, knee deep in the thick bunch grass that has filled and glossed their flanks. The muted sound of the animals' neck bells rolls across the water and into our riverboat cabin as they walk the watery buffet, selecting only the most delectable plants.

Soon Ra burns lower in the sky and the Nile is turning dark, slapping our hull with halfhearted splashes. The distant green trees are now black silhouettes. Dinner will be served shortly in the ship's dining room so Sara and I take turns freshening up before leaving the room. Our cabin is on the second floor of the ship, closest to the main lobby, which means we step out of our door and almost immediately arrive at the top of a wide, dramatic wooden staircase—complete with an ornate carpet runner—which curves down to the main floor lobby facing the reception desk. Fore and aft of the tall desk, on opposite sides of the lobby, are entrances to the dining room and the lounge, respectively. One wall perpendicular to the desk features the gangway doors we use for shore excursions. The other wall features tall picture windows fitted with upholstered bench seating.

We double back under the staircase and into the dining room. It hasn't yet started to fill with guests and we have an assortment of unoccupied tables to choose from.

"How about this one?" I've selected an empty four-top table along the perimeter of the room and I place my backpack on the chair nearest the window. Sara hangs her bag on the chair opposite mine. Then we head to the buffet to fill our plates.

Returning to the table I see someone has hung their purse on the chair next to mine and wonder who we will have the pleasure of visiting with at dinner. Perhaps the two Australian women (if we're lucky!) or the young couple from the Bay Area, or one of the lovely ladies traveling alone, Veronica or Ebony or Kelly?

We have scarcely placed our plates on the table and taken our seats when we can't help but notice two waiters nearby in hushed discussion. They are trying not to look at our table but are obviously looking at our table.

"Hello," a tall waiter with a name tag that says Youssef approaches and greets us. It is invariably Youssef who serves our table and he makes no effort to hide his infatuation with me.

"Would you like some American coffee?" he asks.

The other morning Youssef noticed my displeasure with the Nescafe packets and from nowhere seemed to conjure up a cup of freshly brewed "American-style" coffee, which he offered with the demeanor of someone proposing marriage. Though I'm single and open to a relationship,

Youssef's feelings are doomed to remain unrequited; I've no attraction to him in that way. But there's no reason to be rude, especially when tomorrow's real coffee is on the line.

"La, shukren," (no, thank you in Egyptian Arabic) I respond. "I would like a glass of the Sauvignon Blanc. The white wine," I clarify, pointing to the menu.

Sara orders a glass of wine as well and Youssef leaves to fulfill our wishes. Just then Michael arrives at the table with Steve, the sweet Australian man who we discover has participated in a number of Michael's previous journeys. They're both carrying plates of food and I motion to the handbag saving the chair Michael is about to take. He seems not to care and sits down anyway.

"Hello," he smiles as he places his plate on the table and I realize it's his man-bag that has been on the chair all along.

"Hello," I respond. "Hi, Steve."

Youssef returns to the table and places my wine before me. He is visibly perturbed that the men have joined us.

"Shukren, Youssef," I offer, hoping the use of his name will soften the blow. He moves to the other side of the table and serves Sara her wine before moving away in silence.

"You know, he's quite smitten with you," Michael teases.

"I know," I respond. "But he is not going to be visiting my sacred site."

Sara giggles.

"They think I'm your father," Michael continues with a twinkle in his eye, "I've been offered forty camels for you."

"Only forty!" I retort indignantly, "I must be losing it. I think I'm worth at least seventy."

The table blooms with laughter, causing the other diners to lift their heads toward us.

"Well, you know these middle–eastern men prefer women with a little more meat on their bones," Sara razzes. For maybe the first time ever, her full figure has been complimented more than mine since we've been in Egypt. A chuckle of consensus bounces around the table.

"I know. I must look like a skinny white skeleton next to these voluptuous Egyptian women," I concede.

I'm actually very happy for Sara but I'm starting to feel the teeniest bit ganged up on. When one is slim, the "meat on your bones," comment gets really old. Imagine a skinny person telling a heavy woman she needs to take some meat off her bones!

"OK then," I offer a friendly challenge to the table, "Where will I do well?"

Michael turns to me. "You're looking pretty perfect from where I'm sitting."

The table goes silent. Sara takes a long sip of her wine. "Of course," he continues, "one can't get involved with the people on the trip. It's against the rules," he explains cheerfully as if it's a purely theoretical conversation.

"Of course," I smile back, savoring the chemistry. Michael has been a perfect gentleman and the innocuous, good-natured flirting is a welcome and fun surprise for a single lady who supports her own household at home and regretfully, has little time for dating.

The conversation rollicks on, easy and in the moment. Steve is beyond charming and hilarious, like so many Aussies are. He and Michael have a deep comfort level with one another, which they graciously invite us to share. Before long I am wiping away tears of laughter and the dishes are being cleared.

"Better get to bed early," Michael advises, "We're going to leave for Edfu before dawn."

"Okay!" I sign our ticket and Sara and I collect our bags.

"Goodnight."

"Goodnight."

"G'nite Mate."

Sara and I leave the men at the table and walk up the grand staircase and into our cabin. Tossing my bag on the bed, I open the tiny slider, feeling a rush of heavy warm air. The ship is underway and in the darkness beyond our balcony, I hear the Nile river flowing past. I flick on the small outdoor lamp, hoping to get a glimpse of the water but instead I see a cloud of buzzing visitors around the light bulb. The dreaded Nile mosquitoes! They of the biblical plague. The words West Nile Virus take on a new dimension of reality, and I quickly slide and latch the door. While I pull the curtains closed, Sara fiddles with the air conditioner. Soon, a faint chill blows gently from the grate and we each settle into our cozy cots. There are no televisions in these rooms, so we open up the books about Egypt we have brought. Snuggling into the modest but clean bed linens, I scan my book's index for Edfu to study up for tomorrow's excursion to the Temple of Horus.

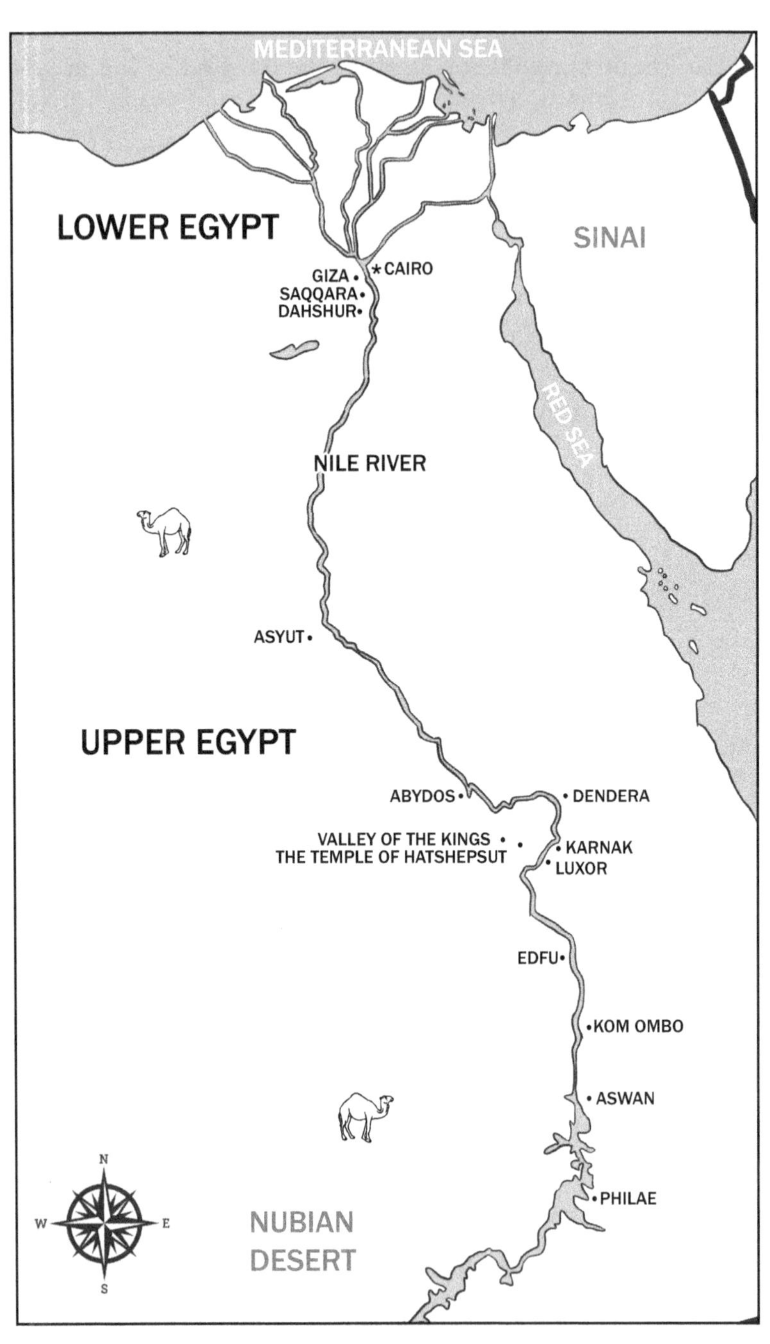

MEDITERRANEAN SEA
LOWER EGYPT
SINAI
GIZA
SAQQARA
DAHSHUR
CAIRO
RED SEA
NILE RIVER
ASYUT
UPPER EGYPT
ABYDOS
DENDERA
VALLEY OF THE KINGS
THE TEMPLE OF HATSHEPSUT
KARNAK
LUXOR
EDFU
KOM OMBO
ASWAN
PHILAE
NUBIAN
DESERT
N
W
E
S

Chapter 20

THE TEMPLE OF HORUS

I awake to shouting and the strange commotion of horse and car sounds mixed together. I'm sleeping on the bed nearest our tiny cabin's glass balcony door so I sit up and reach the twelve or so inches to peek through the curtains.

We are docked next to a busy boulevard and under the street lights are horse carriages lined bumper to bumper for as far as I can see. And they are close! The indigo glow reveals the location of our cabin has positioned us exactly at street level. It feels as if we could just walk out on our balcony and step onto the sidewalk. I dare not open the fabric any wider for privacy purposes. My activity has awakened Sara and I'm trying to convey the improbable proximity of what I'm seeing. She's a larger woman but still tries to position herself between my bed and the slider for a look through the drapes. What a sight she would be for the carriage drivers lining the road with her short cotton nightgown and goddess-worthy cleavage!

"I'll put the kettle on for the coffee," I announce, rising from my bed. We've developed a casual, unspoken schedule for preparing the in-room coffee service. Each of us receives morning coffee delivered to their bed on alternating days. Today it is my turn to serve.

The instant, organic, travel-packet coffee I've packed makes a hot and effective libation, but it's no match for Youssef's freshly brewed cup and even more lowly compared to a bespoke Turkish coffee served strong and steaming, fragrant with cardamom and a hint of sugar. Luckily, we can get the latter in the ship's dining room, but we're running late for the early morning call time.

After a quick breakfast we walk up the gangplank to the boulevard and are assigned a horse carriage which will take us to the Temple of Horus. The anonymous driver gives the horse a click and a crack of the reins and we are off, trotting bumpily down the road, passing and then being passed by other galloping carriages jockeying for position. I wrap my neck in a linen scarf and watch the trees and shops pass by in the sapphire pre-dawn light. The stores are not yet open but I spy a few I wouldn't mind checking out later, inshallah. I'm trying not to obsess over the narrow neck and sharp hip bones of the scrawny bay mare that's pulling our carriage. Her blinders prevent me from looking at her eyes, but I notice she clips along without the use of the driver's whip and her ears are pricked attentively forward. I've owned and trained horses for years (the magazine I founded in 2009 is titled *COWGIRL*) and my heart breaks for both the service animals and the operators. For years, the tourist numbers in Egypt have been below what's needed to support the good people dependent on the industry and the beasts of burden dependent on them.

I'm reminded of a charity my sister told me about, a team of volunteers made up of a veterinarian, a farrier, a leather craftsmen and so on, who travel the world and serve the needs of working animals. They shoe and worm carriage horses, repair and adjust ill-fitting saddles or harnesses that have rubbed a furry patient raw, treat teeth and wounds, and provide just about whatever is needed with no cost, and just as importantly, no judgment. Animal-dependent entrepreneurs in some countries may make less in a week or month than we spend for a latte at home, so they can't be blamed for choosing to feed a family over buying new tack or medicine for their horses. I make a mental commitment to do more research on the organization once I'm back home.

When we arrive in the wide plaza that is the gathering place for entering the Temple of Horus, the sky goddess has not yet birthed Ra into being for the day. High above, nearly invisible stars still glitter faintly in Nut's deep blue body which is lightening up by the moment. High atop the cliffs that border the walkway to the temple, a lone dog stands in silhouette, as if the symbolic Opener of the Way.

The sun rises, and the first pylon of the Temple of Horus reveals itself in its gigantic glory. The two massive walls that make up the pylon are 118 feet tall, each featuring giant-sized carved reliefs that show Ptolemy XII holding an enemy by the hair, soon to be smited with the Pharaoh's raised club in front of the falcon-headed god Horus. The Ptolemies (pronounced Toll-em-ees) were Egyptian-born Greek rulers who took control of Egypt in the last few centuries BCE. The last, Ptolemy XII, Neos Dionysus, was succeeded by Cleopatra.

Though Ptolemy XII's violent propaganda is a visitor's first impression of Edfu, this temple was built neither for him nor by him. Ptolemy II began the project and must have imagined a time when the ancient knowledge would be lost, for he inscribed along a temple wall the detailed story of the *Aku Shemshu Hor* (Shining Ones, Followers of Horus). These giant, god-like people arrived after the great flood and taught the ancients precise and proper templemaking, as well as astronomy, agriculture, medicine, and virtuous living. Described as 'humanlike, but not totally human,' some people believe the Followers of Horus, The Shining Ones, may have actually been extra-terrestrials. Others say they were the survivors of Atlantis.

We don't know what Ptolemy II's motivations were but we do know that in 280 BCE, he commissioned the priest-scribe Manatheo to write down the entire history of Egypt. Without this text—and Herodotus' travelogue of Egypt penned during the Twenty-Seventh Dynasty (during the years 525-404 BCE)—our knowledge of ancient Egypt would be vastly different. When Ptolemy II rebuilt this massive temple dedicated to Horus, Hathor, and their child Ihy in 50 BCE, he sited it on the original primeval mound consecrated by the gods at the beginning of time, what the Egyptians called *Zep Tepi*.

After seeing the monument's holy of holies where the granite shrine—an artifact from one of the temple's earlier incarnations—once showcased a golden statue of Horus, I've wandered off and discovered a narrow, enclosed masonry staircase. Fortunately or unfortunately, the sprawling grounds and lack of tourists have created an unexpected opportunity. Exploring alone inside ancient dark temple passages is hard to describe. My feet tread stone steps worn smooth by the sandals of kings and priestesses, maybe even Cleopatra herself. The rock walls and ceiling are covered with images and hieroglyphs. My eyes take them in, but they are so remarkable I have to remind myself these are real, ancient Egyptian carvings. My hand slides along a smooth wall carved with a handsome naked god, penis erect. Farther up, an elaborate rectangular ark is depicted, complete with it's long carrying handles. The Ark of the Covenant? Maybe, but I always forget arks are originally Egyptian.

With the silly freedom born of complete and utter solitude, I decide to engage the carvings. Returning to the handsome god, I ask the neters silently for a lover who is spiritual, kind, and fun, someone who can feel the mystery in places like these. It is believed that in Egypt's golden, predynastic times, the flesh and blood goddess Hathor actually visited her hawk-headed consort Horus here at this very temple. I imagine Horus and Hathor climbing these steps hand in hand to a rooftop tryst, where only the sky could watch. We do know that in historic times a large statue of Hathor was floated from her temple at Dendera to this temple, where the stone lovers were symbolically reunited. David Rosalie writes: The Edfu site is the largest temple dedicated to Horus and Hathor of Dendera. It was the center of several festivals sacred to Horus. Each year, "Hathor travelled south from her temple at Dendera to visit Horus at

Edfu, and this event marking their sacred marriage was the occasion of a great festival and pilgrimage."[32]

At the ark, I spontaneously turn around and step backwards towards the carving until my back is making contact with the wall. Immediately, I'm zapped with a strange energy, shaking uncontrollably for a few seconds before I separate myself from the stone. I am, literally, shocked.

In my childhood home the bathroom with the shower was across a small hallway from the clothes dryer. One day after putting some towels in the appliance to warm up, I stepped from the shower dripping wet to grab one. I accidentally touched the dryer drum and got buzzed. That's what this felt like. It wasn't the crackling little white shock that sometimes happens when you touch someone or something. It was a quick but distinct vibrating jolt. As if my back had accidentally touched an electric fence. Within moments my body stopped shuddering, but the electricity—or whatever it was—continued to jitter through my cells like a triple espresso.

---

[32]Rosalie, David. 1993. *Discovering Ancient Egypt.* Facts on File, NY, NY p. 99.

Chapter 21

Spa Day
on the Riverboat

Riding the bus back to the Nile we learn that our afternoon is unscheduled! Sara and I decide to use the opportunity to enjoy the riverboat's open air swimming pool and schedule a massage. The pool is on the uppermost deck which we discover is covered entirely in a faded green faux-grass carpet. What the flooring lacks in style is more than made up for by it's silky, foot-friendly texture and the fact that it stays comfortable to walk on in 110 degree heat. The aft portion of the deck is densely populated by tubular steel and teak dining sets surrounding a blonde wood bar—all empty. I think Sara and I are the only people crazy enough to come up here in this heat, which I'm told is unseasonably hot even for Egypt. I notice a coffee urn on the deserted bar and realize this is the secret location where Youssef sourced the "American style" percolated coffee he courted me with at breakfast. The entire bar area is shaded by a canopy, however the front half of the ship, including the blunted bow which holds the small pool, is entirely exposed to Ra's intense, unblinking gaze.

I'm leaning back with my legs dangling off smooth lapis-colored tiles that form a wide ledge a few inches below the water level, creating a shallow sunning area before meeting the pool's deeper depths. It reminds me of the platforms captive dolphins and whales slide up onto to pose for the audience. I have trained captive dolphins in Florida and interacted with wild dolphins in the Bahamas, California, and the Amazon and I believe these sentient creatures should never be incarcerated for entertainment and profit. But that is a cause for another day.

Today, I am sailing the Nile. I look around, enchanted by the moment. Beyond the ship's railing in every direction flows the gentle, life-giving river. Stiff, emerald-colored reeds and thick, waist-high grasses clothe her distant banks. Beyond the grasses, dense crowds of deep green date palms lean in toward her fertile shores. Behind us, the ship's wake rocks out toward the riverbank. I imagine its rhythmic lapping against her sacred littoral. And everywhere I look, there is Ra.

"I'm going in," I announce to Sara before slipping off the ledge and into the pool like a show-weary cetacean.

Sara's sitting on a pool-side chaise behind me, putting on sunscreen and adjusting her hat. I try to think back to the last time I swam in a pool. It's been a long time and I'm in a buoyant, lighthearted mood. I grew up surfing on the California coast but I live inland now, in a much colder climate. There may be snow on the ground when I get home. I feel like I'm in a dream.

"Are you coming in?" I've treaded water out to the deepest region of the pool which is over my 5' 4" frame. Sliding sideways through the water until I can just feel the bottom, I start to slowly tiptoe to the shallows.

"I'm going to read for awhile," Sara responds, lifting her book as evidence. It's a non-fiction tome about ancient temples and long-lost civilizations. Just then, Michael arrives to the pool deck, towel in hand.

"Hello Darling," I greet Michael playfully from the pool.

"Oh, *Darling* is it now?" he smiles, placing his towel and sunglasses on a nearby chaise.

Several more guests have joined me in the pool, three young people in their twenties or thirties. They look like locals. There are two women and a man. One of the girls and the guy are obviously a couple. The other woman must be a friend or sister. The couple have dipped in near me and the woman resurfaces first. Her large eyes, smooth skin, and high cheekbones look like they could have come off a temple wall.

"Oh, you're so beautiful," I gasp. Her coffee-colored

skin, black hair, and tiger-eye irises are the opposite of my Irish complexion. Not to mention the many more trips I've taken around the sun.

"Thank you," she replies, clearly flattered. Her man is beaming.

"*She's* beautiful? What about me?" Michael complains loudly, rising from his lounge chair. I realize we are all so close everyone can hear everyone else.

"And you're very handsome," I play along, proffering the fished-for compliment.

Michael's taking off his shirt to get in the pool. I make a point of looking away. Sara glances at me over her sunglasses.

Two other participants from Michael's tour have come on the scene: Elle, a lovely, intelligent young woman who I think is a filmmaker and Kurt, a physician who is traveling with his wife who is also a doctor. Kurt is a talkative Texan and he is standing waist deep in the pool with Michael making a case for something, I'm not sure what. Elle has staked out a chaise a few rows back from the pool and put in some earbuds. Sara has come down and seated herself on the side of the pool and is splashing herself to cool off. I swim up and pull myself out onto the pool edge near her. For just a instant, the water droplets on my skin chill cold from the wind's caress, then they evaporate into the hot Egyptian sky.

"It's almost 4:30" Sara exclaims. "We're going to be late for our massages!"

The onboard spa was able to accommodate two massage appointments at 4:30 p.m. which we eagerly booked. I clamber to my feet and step over the poolside edge and onto the soft, faux grass. Wrapping my hair in a towel, I realize it's almost dry already and abandon the terrycloth on a nearby chaise to locate my room key. Then I pull my red maxi dress over my head (she of the Queen Hatshepsut story) and we head down to our cabin to get out of our wet swimsuits and into the ship's spa.

Now it is 4:30 and we can't figure out where to go because the directions to the spa have led us to an unmarked door on the far side of the riverboat. We are hopelessly lost.

"This is where they said to go," Sara bemoans.

I just shrug and keep looking. It can't be easy to hide a whole spa. It's got to be somewhere down one of these hallways.

I'm poking my head around a corner when a gregarious young Egyptian woman seems to manifest out of nowhere.

"Do you have massage appointments?"

"Yes!"

"Come this way, please."

We follow her toward the spa but wind up back at the same unmarked door, which she unlocks. Inside are two massage tables pushed up against opposite sides of the room, which leaves about a foot of space in between them. It's kind of like our cabin except the starboard wall of the cramped room features a wide window with a view of the Nile. The other interior wall is windowless. There is no reception desk, no decor, no sink or bathroom, not really enough room for one massage table, let alone two. Nevertheless, I am instructed to take off my clothes and lie on the windowless-wall bed, face down.

"But leave your underwear on," our mistress warns, straightening the sheets, "And your bra too."

"And you over here," she instructs Sara, motioning to the other massage table whose edge is literally touching the glass window. Faded cotton half-curtains are tugged almost closed over the window to protect us from the river's eyes.

"OK, Habibi, I'll be back," the woman says as she closes the door behind her. When used platonically, *Habibi* is similar to "sweetheart" or "honey." It can also mean "beloved" or "darling."

"Did you book us a couple's massage?" I tease Sara. I'm trying to get undressed and under the sheet but she keeps backing into me, trying to get her shoes off. We're both giggling.

"No, they said they could accommodate two massages if we didn't mind having them at the same time," she confesses, laughing.

Eventually we get settled, and not a moment too soon. There is a knock on the door.

"Are you ready?"

"Yes."

In comes our Habibi, along with an Egyptian masseur who sets about tucking in my sheets like a pro. Ah, no wonder I had to keep my underwear on. I'm surprised to have a male massage therapist in a Muslim country. But it's fine with me.

Massage oil is rubbed between palms and then onto our thankful bodies. My massage is quite skillfully conducted. Heavenly, actually. I make a mental note that I should treat myself more often. There is a lot of Arabic being bandied about however, and it eventually comes out that Habibi, who is Sara's therapist, is concerned that her legs are becoming swollen from the unforgiving heat. After a bit of advice on how to reduce puffy calves (I eavesdrop with interest) the room becomes silent.

Then more indecipherable Egyptian Arabic. Habibi leaves Sara and I feel her approach. She unhooks my bra and tucks the sheets under my upper arms to conceal any side-breast view. Then my fella resumes the massage, working on my now truly naked upper back. Apparently, the masseur is not allowed to unhook the bra, but massaging a braless woman seems to be permitted. After a thorough (and very professional) back massage, Habibi is once again called to rehook my bra, after which the classic massage sheet-curtain is raised and I flip onto my back. The massage continues without further incident until, regrettably, our hour has passed.

"Ok, we are finished," Habibi announces to us both. I am thankful because sometimes, especially when you don't speak the same language, it's hard to know. "You get a free facial today," she continues.

Free facial?

"Stay here," she says, "lay under the sheet on your backs."

They both leave the room.

"We get a free facial?" I look incredulously to Sara. I don't see how it would be possible to receive a facial in this room. She just makes a funny face.

Knock, knock. The therapists both re-enter the room carrying bowls heaped with what looks like guacamole. I guess my fella doesn't speak a word of English because Habibi speaks for both of them, as she has done all afternoon.

"This is a mask with special ingredients for your skin that will make it very soft and smooth. These are Egyptian ingredients that detoxify and rejuvenate your skin. Special mud. All natural ingredients."

Oooh, OK. I'm all in.

We lay back and our faces are gently cleansed and then slathered with the guac-stuff, which smells earthy and herbal and fresh. The consistency, however, is exactly like good, hand-made guacamole—thick, green, and lumpy. Then they leave again and we lay back, allowing the magic to happen. Almost immediately, the masks start drying and tightening considerably.

Now the masks are definitely dry but there is no sign

of our wellness therapists.

"How much longer, do you think?" I'm starting to get hungry and I'm ready to get dressed and leave.

"I don't know," Sara offers. "But my mask is definitely ready to be removed."

So we wait. And we wait. And we wait some more.

Eventually, Habibi returns and seems surprised that we're still here.

"Oh, you're done." She says.

"What about the masks?" Sara inquires.

"Leave them on another ten minutes then wash them off in your room. Please get dressed now and go."

The door closes. I look at Sara. Her face is covered in an extremely thick layer of what looks like dried equine snot. It dawns on me that I must look the same, and that our cabin is the very closest room to the grand lobby and majestic curving staircase, which means we have to walk through the entire, most crowded public area of the ship to reach it. I shriek with laughter.

We laugh until we cry. Then we get dressed and scurry like ship rats around the back of the boat and down a dark hallway clearly meant for the ship's employees. We are now at the ships draft line, where a couple of Egyptian men are standing in a cargo-style door open to the river, smoking cigarettes. Continuing through another obscure hallway, we find some stairs that connect back up to the guest cabin deck and finally, to the dimly lit corridor leading to our room. From here we can clandestinely access our cabin door from the direction opposite the exposed grand staircase. We dash for our room and I furtively unlock the door. Safely inside, we flop down on the beds in hysterics.

"I'm going to go wash this off."

"No!" Sara shouts. " I want to take a picture. No one is going to believe this!"

The lighting in our cabin is not bright, but the sun still hangs low in the sky, so we open the slider door and lean out onto our diminutive balcony where Ra lights our lumpy green faces and laughs.

Chapter 22

KOM OMBO

Flying south, high above the river valley, a falcon cocks his head and follows the lapis lazuli necklace of the Nile draped between the historical temples of Upper Egypt. To the east, the imposing columns and sky-piercing obelisks of Dendera, Karnak, and Luxor slide silently under his left wing. To the west, in the Valley of the Kings, the spirits of the Pharaohs have long since reunited with their *Ba* (souls). Above the necropolis the sacred goddess-mountain Dehenet rises, wishing godspeed upon the falcon's wingbeats as he passes her rocky slopes. Farther south, the tiercel catches a thermal, spiraling higher and higher until he is over four thousand feet above the land of Khem—invisible to earthbound eyes—before starting an elegant, effortless descent.

Down the falcon slides, riding the whistling wind beneath his stiff wings, toward the edges of Upper Egypt. Caught by a pang of nostalgia, the handsome bird finds himself circling the temple at Edfu, remembering his beloved Hathor and their passionate couplings in the temple's holy of holies, first as flesh and blood lovers, then later as stone statues ritually reunited by their followers. With love in his breast, the falcon flies on.

Farther south, where Egyptian culture has blended and clashed and blended again with the proud Nubians, the tired falcon alights on a tall temple frieze. Below his talons, a sun disk flanked by two cobras is carved in relief on the limestone facade. The raptor folds his wings and rests. He is comfortable here, in his temple, or more accurately his *half* of the temple.

This is Kom Ombo, a monument of both darkness and light. This one building includes two temples. The north half is dedicated to Horus, or Heru, the golden solar falcon (from whom we get the word hero). The temple's south portion reflects the shadow side and is dedicated to Sobek, the primeval crocodile god.

*** *

The group I'm traveling with has left our docked cruise ship to walk the riverside promenade that leads to Kom Ombo temple. After passing the peculiar attraction that is the crocodile mummy museum, my falconer's instincts catch sight of what looks like a peregrine flying overhead. I'm not even sure if peregrine falcons are found in this region. Could it be a Lanner or Barbary falcon, or some kind of North African kite? To stop walking, even for a moment of bird-watching, invites the relentless attention of the riverside vendors so the only recourse is to just keep moving. I dodge and weave through the sales assault but I'm happy to see the shopkeepers' nets have caught some customers. These hard-working men will have some valuable American dollars to take home to their families tonight. My falcon, however, is long gone.

At the monument kiosk, in what has become a familiar ritual, my backpack is screened and the left edge of my Kom Ombo Temple & Crocodile Museum ticket is carefully torn off, awarding me entry. Climbing the wide limestone steps to the front courtyard, I am delighted to see my little falcon perched on the roof of the temple, above a carving of a sun disk flanked by two cobras. Having years of experience sitting Saudi-style with my own falcon on my knee, I can read the bird's body language. I notice, even from this distance, that it's a tiercel (male falcon). He's relaxed, with one foot drawn up to its belly. As our group approaches, however, I see him stand up straight and waggle his tail feathers and I know what's coming. With one powerful stroke of his long tapered wings, the falcon knifes into the air and sweeps away on the breeze. Squinting into the sun, I imagine I see him turn his head back and look at me.

Horus?

Horus, the Golden Falcon, the son of Isis and Osiris, the last Egyptian god born on earth's soil. The great hero who in pre-dynastic times brought goodness and cohesion back to Egypt after the murder of his father by his destructive uncle Set. This was ten thousand years ago, when a race of human-like 'gods' ruled the land. The original pantheon is said to have been born from the sky, and the sky herself is a goddess called Nut.

Stories of sorcery and shape-shifting, of sem priests lifting multi-ton stones using sound and speaking 'spells' that could heal or curse, all these are credited to the neteru (plural for neter). They were brilliant and powerful, but apparently not immune to drama and suffering. They somehow seem almost human, or rather, we humans seem very much like them. The ancients were convinced that the neters were here on Earth with us, in the flesh. And then they left, but not without a trace.

The Akhu Shemsu Hor ('Shining Ones, Followers of Horus') were a semi-divine group of sages, priests, and priestesses who still ruled Egypt until, as the Greek historian Herodotus was informed, the first fully-human king was installed. This first Pharaoh of a 'purely human bloodline' was Menes. The year was 3,100 BCE.

Are Egypt's fantastical stories simply beyond belief? I think we have made them so because confronting the truth shatters our worldview. Anyone who has been inside the Great Pyramid or even stands at its base can tell you this thing is important. Some thing or some one was on our earth, possessing a technology for working stone that is so beyond our comprehension, we simply ignore it. It's as if our collective mind is blocking a traumatic truth. We have been taught fear, but the temples are patient.

Kom Ombo has been patiently waiting for me. The

three majestic columns at the front of this temple form two pathways into the sacred building. At the time the temple was in use, initiates were tested to see which door they chose. One side represented the higher self, the solar energy, if you will. This was the side dedicated to Horus. The other option represented the darker elements of experience, unmanifest potential, perhaps confusion. This is the Sobek side, dedicated to the fierce, devouring crocodile god.

Sobek is both good and evil, depending on who you ask. Some scholars believe Sobek means "to collect" or to "bring together".[33] An apt name for a deity whose temple features towering stones linking life's two eternal paths. The dual entry's central pillar is shared by the two opposing stone doorways.

In a modern recreation of the ancient initiate's challenge, Michael stepped back and asked us to choose our portal. I knew the story of the temple, I saw the falcon, and I knew without a doubt which side to go through. Not surprisingly, our whole group of spiritual, sacred-sites travelers walked forward to the left "positive" entrance. Which is why I was utterly surprised to find myself walking though the other passageway!

I had made the decision in an instant, or maybe I didn't make the decision at all. I knew it was the dark side. What I didn't know was that several of the other women in our group had followed me. Later they would tell me they trusted my judgment as a leader and thought I would choose the correct door.

---

[33]Houston, Jean. 1995. *The Passion of Isis and Osiris.* Ballantine/ Wellspring (Random House), NY, p. 359.

Like the great collector Sobek, Michael gathered us round and revealed the nature of the two entrances. Much happy twittering. He asked who had chosen the shadow side and I sheepishly raised my hand along with my two unfortunate disciples. There was no going anonymous, everyone had seen us. Graciously, he espoused the necessary nature of both sides. Walking through the dark door meant we might be working on meaningful internal challenges or dealing with disappointing beliefs, or something like that anyway. I think the gist was that we weren't actually evil people. I couldn't really hear over the nervous beating of my heart. The stifling Egyptian air had become hard to breathe. My ego flushed with an unfamiliar feeling of shame.

What no one could have known, except the Kom Ombo temple, was that in the months preceding the trip, I was in the clammy grip of the proverbial dark night of the soul. Despite being totally blissed out by the realization of a literally lifelong obsession to visit Egypt, in real life I had been battling serious disillusionment and depression.

In the decade and a half prior, I had created a new, second marriage and a new publishing company. Within a few years, the magazine I founded was sold in sixteen countries around the world. I reveled in the feeling that I had created something from nothing, and thoroughly enjoyed the creative responsibilities of the business, not to mention the complimentary travel and high-end hotel suites offered to the Editor-in-Chief of an upscale magazine. Within a few more years I wanted out, badly. I had achieved everything I aspired to, but my spiritual trajectory—my energy signature—was scraping painfully up against the conservative element of my readership. I needed to break up with my magazine. But I didn't know how to get out. So I stayed.

It wasn't all bad, of course. I delighted in embedding magic in the magazine pages through symbolic writing and images. I intended to inspire, to celebrate beauty and people and places. Subscribers wrote me and told me I succeeded. But it came at a cost. I remember flipping my pillow at all hours of the night, trying to will myself into unconsciousness. As soon as my head touched the case, the upcoming print run, or the next issue's shipping costs, or the commissions due my advertising staff would run through my mind like a ticker tape turned red. Most concerning was the fact that media as a whole was transitioning to electronic delivery. The margins for an independent paper magazine publisher dependent on advertising dollars were getting shaved thinner than the fresh Parmesan at the Four Seasons' chef's table.

I acquired a business partner who shored up the magazine financially, but satisfying a broader readership meant moving farther away from my vision. I was introduced to the dirty little not-so-secret of native advertising. This is when an advertiser pays a magazine to create what looks and reads like editorial content, but is actually designed to sell a certain product or service. All the big magazines were doing it, and once my advertisers and my business partner got a taste, my editorial integrity quickly bled out.

Emotionally and creatively exhausted, I eventually sold the magazine after nine years of publishing. I was debt-free, but with only about a year's salary as compensation. I felt farther away from my purpose than ever. Ok, I told the Universe. I am ready to transform. My spiritual mastery is my highest priority and I'm willing to give up anything and everything that's keeping me from it. Apparently, having money and a husband was keeping me from it.

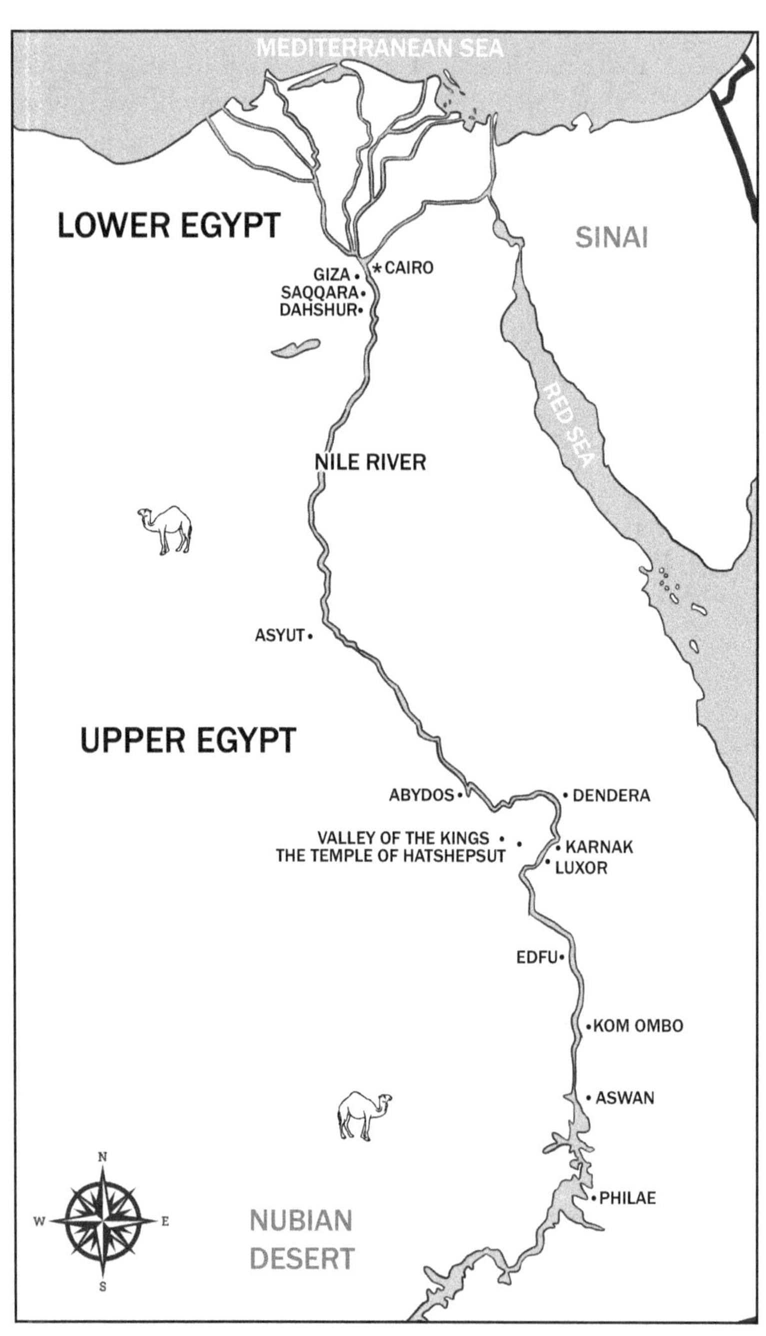

MEDITERRANEAN SEA
LOWER EGYPT
SINAI
GIZA
SAQQARA
DAHSHUR
*CAIRO
RED SEA
NILE RIVER
ASYUT
UPPER EGYPT
ABYDOS
DENDERA
VALLEY OF THE KINGS
THE TEMPLE OF HATSHEPSUT
KARNAK
LUXOR
EDFU
KOM OMBO
ASWAN
PHILAE
N
W
E
S
NUBIAN
DESERT

Chapter 23

Last Man Dancing

The Kom Ombo temple's link to the crocodile God Sobek was not purely metaphoric. Until fairly recent times, this area of the Nile was swarming with large crocs. Some of these reptiles were kept in captivity—and in traditional Nubian households, they still are. It is said that initiates studying at Kom Ombo temple had to prove they could overcome their fear by swimming with the crocodiles. Stories say that the temple courtyard had a large pool filled with water and (presumably well-fed) crocodiles. Each adept was tasked with sprinting across the sleeping creatures' backs and placing a gold earring in one of the reptile's ears. Nile crocodiles do have small ear flaps over their ear openings, a fact which makes this outlandish tale at least anatomically possible.

After leaving the Kom Ombo temple and despite my better judgment, I find myself touring the crocodile museum (my ticket includes admission to both attractions). Attraction may not be the right word. Anyone who has walked a humid, indoor reptile exhibit at a large zoo can recall the inimitable fragrance of captive snakes and large lizards that permeates the sticky atmosphere. It's a strong but tolerable odor until one adds in the fact that the specimens in the Kom Ombo crocodile museum have long since died. Their desiccated corpses lay side by side inside a central glass room, shrunken and soulless. Visitors circumnavigate the axis of the exhibit via a dark hallway with scant (but appreciated) air conditioning. These are big crocs, and I scan their shriveled heads to find any glint of gold. It appears none of these unlucky creatures contributed to an aspiring mage's mastery.

A nearby display case showcases several crocs still swaddled in their mummification cloths, revealing the ancient method of preservation. Three hundred of these reptilian mummies were found in proximity to the temple! Farther in, an especially sad exhibit contains a selection of torn leathery eggs, revealing the kitten-sized skeletons of never-born Nile crocodiles. A handsome stone carving of two crocodiles, fleshy and fierce, over a carved image of Hathor is a welcome distraction from the harsh, natural history reality. It might be a limestone block from the Kom Ombo temple, for I found out that Hathor was honored with her own chapel here. Or maybe it's granite. I'd like to know more, but the cloying smell of mummified herps mixed with the odor of sweaty, unfamiliar humans drives me out of the crocodile museum.

Arriving back at the Kom Ombo temple entrance—the rendezvous point for our group of modern initiates—I see everyone is descending the spacious front steps toward an open air shisha bar conveniently set up at the bottom of the campus. Shisha is the tobacco, often flavored, that is smoked from a water pipe (hookah) via a tube and mouthpiece. Smartly dressed Egyptian men in long-sleeved western shirts and trousers lounge in chairs around the periphery of the lantern-lit courtyard, holding their hookah mouthpieces to their lips. The tall ornamental pipes stand beside their chairs like shiny brass butlers. In the central area, where woven brown umbrellas with beaded fringe create an organic ceiling over the many tables, a cadre of hookah pipes is being prepared for patrons, filled with fresh shisha and fitted with disposable plastic mouthpieces.

"Here Miss," a lanky Egyptian waiter wearing sharp cheekbones and a traditional fez pulls out a sturdy cane chair from the long line of tables that has been pushed together for our group.

"Shukren," I arrange the flamenco-flared hemline of my cotton skirt forward under my thighs and slip into the chair. The comfortable, oversized cushions remind me that I've been on my feet for hours.

I'm barely seated when the peer pressure starts to suck on one of these humongous hookahs. A chorus of try its, you should do its, and oh come ons is bantered around the table. Several of the men and my travel buddy Sara need no encouragement to partake. Soon, the chairside pipes are ceremoniously placed beside those so inclined. I enjoy watching the exotic perniciousness, but I have absolutely no desire to smoke.

I call the waiter over in Arabic, which impresses everyone at the table including myself. I had no idea if the sounds I was making would be recognized as the "Excuse me" I intended.

"Turkish coffee please."

"Of course, Miss. How much sugar?"

"Medium."

Sara is at the head of the table puffing away like the caterpillar in Alice In Wonderland, the cafe band is warming up to play, and I am starting to relax. The crowded table is chattering, but I'm just sitting back, taking in the moment. The melodies and rhythms of the traditional Egyptian music are familiar to me, but I've never heard it played like this before, by Egyptians, in Egypt.

Maqsoum, Saidi, Ayoub. I recognize the drumbeats I've taught my Egyptian dance students many times. I've even played them myself. But to hear them now, on the banks of the Nile, is like being in a dream. Nursing my dainty cup of rich, cardamon-laced coffee, I let the awkwardness of my wrong choice at the temple doors be drummed out by the tabla and carried up and away, like a feather dancing on the warm wind. As if releasing the jesses of a trusted falcon, I set my affronted ego free to fly away. I know she will return, but hopefully with more of the far-sighted wisdom of Horus. Maybe one day we will have served each other just enough, so that we can both be utterly and eternally free.

Shouts and yips pierce the air. I sit up and take notice. The band is traveling around the restaurant, cajoling patrons to participate. Michael, a former rock star and musician, is handed an exotic string instrument. The "Fiddle of the Nile" is an ancient rabab (string instrument) with a wavering, passionate voice—an ancestor of the violin. Michael stands up and plays but I can't really hear over the clapping, shaking of tambourines, and singing. One of the musicians tries to pull a mortified woman from her seat to dance. She's made the mistake of taking his hand and rises a few inches off her cushion before snapping back into the safety of her chair, pointing at me.

Over they come, this authentic little Egyptian folk band, singing and drumming. One of the young men offers his hand.

"Would you like to dance?"

"*Aywa*." (Yes)

I don't remember much of the dance, or maybe I remember everything.

There were four of us, the three fellas from the band and myself. I could feel all the customers' eyes upon me, probably thinking they were going to see a silly American make a fool of herself. We were in a circle, our arms woven together, hands on each others' shoulders. The music got slow and obvious, bless their hearts, and they started a classic step and kick. We call it a drop kick in belly dance class. I joined right in, matching the boys and the drumbeats with precision, and even throwing in a little extra hip swivel for good measure. The drummer smiled at me and the music picked right up.

We leaned in and then backwards as our human hoop rotated, using a folk dance step that I also knew. The guys were smiling; they were starting to catch on that this wasn't my first rodeo. I was in belly dancer heaven. Then two of our dancing electrons escaped and took up their instruments, leaving me and the last man dancing. The band seemed to have transformed from the equivalent of a Cheesecake Factory happy birthday gang to passionate performers proud of their musical heritage and having a lot of fun. At least that's what it felt like to me. My human mirror smiled and performed a few moves which I deftly matched, and then that Egyptian fella started to shimmy.

Now this wasn't the Raqs Sharqi shimmy that you see in the late night hotel cabarets. It wasn't all jiggles and shakes. This was a strong, relaxed, very masculine vibrating sort of shimmy. He must have seen the surprise on my face. I had never seen a real Beladi shimmy on a man.

I bent my knees slightly, lifted my arms, took a deep breath and did my best shimmy. Not a super-sexy booty shimmy, not a big look-at-me earthquake hips shimmy, just the most authentic Egyptian shimmy I could pull out. A playful, "I'm not even trying," but hopefully very noticeable hip shimmy.

The crowd clapped and hooted. When we were finished dancing, I made my way back to the table, sweaty and happy. As I wove through the tables, a stylish Egyptian man sitting with his sublime, thinly-veiled girlfriend leaned out of his chair toward me.

"You did very well dancing. You're a good dancer," he said in perfect English with a thick middle eastern accent.

"Shukren," I replied, feeling like Hathor herself.

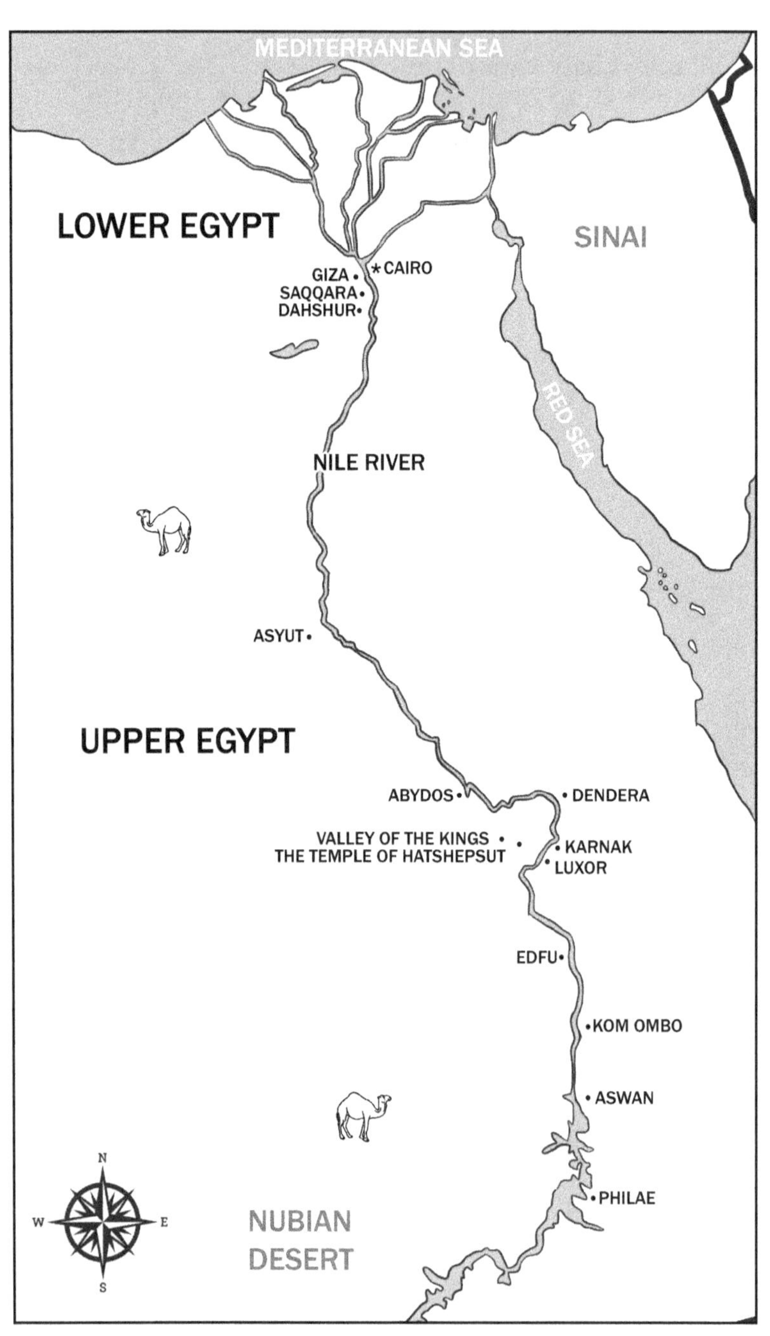

MEDITERRANEAN SEA
LOWER EGYPT
SINAI
GIZA
SAQQARA
DAHSHUR
CAIRO
RED SEA
NILE RIVER
ASYUT
UPPER EGYPT
ABYDOS
DENDERA
VALLEY OF THE KINGS
THE TEMPLE OF HATSHEPSUT
KARNAK
LUXOR
EDFU
KOM OMBO
ASWAN
PHILAE
NUBIAN
DESERT
N
S
E
W

Chapter 24

PAPYRUS
+ VADER

One can only drink in so much wisdom at a time, so, after wandering sacred sights of staggering historical and cultural impact, our itinerary this afternoon includes a palate cleanser of retail therapy. Thankfully, the stores chosen for our visits offer quality, authentic keepsakes like fine jewelry, Egyptian essential oils, and this afternoon, traditionally made papyrus artwork.

Granted, there is a sprinkling of artistically questionable compositions here, but the vast majority of the

Photo: British Library, courtesy of Unsplash

painted papyrus framed and displayed all over the walls is
beautiful, sophisticated, and often features reproductions of
temple scenes or Egyptian myth. From sweeping panoramas
of the post mortem weighing of the heart ceremony in the
Duat, to classical images of Anubis atop an arc, to landscapes
of pyramids, it's all here in vivid color on the inimitable
texture of crushed, cross–woven, vanilla–colored papyrus
fibers.

The proprietor greets us with the sincere delight of
a merchant welcoming a busload of Egypt-obsessed tourists

who can't wait to start shopping. Chilled hibiscus tea in glass cups is offered and we're turned loose to peruse the spacious gallery. In Egypt, it's customary for a merchant to offer mint or hibiscus tea or Turkish coffee to prospective customers, who may sip and chat for some time before consummating the sale. It's a lovely ritual I've come to cherish. Today's clever shopkeeper, however, knowing most westerners don't know how to relax and slow down, encourages us to take our tea "to go" and seek out our purchases from among the hundreds of options on display.

I'm enjoying an elegant papyrus depicting sisters Isis and Nephthys in profile, the rich oranges and golds of their slim dresses enhanced by the flattering studio-style halogen lighting. Isis is reaching back, clasping the hand of her twin. This will be a perfect gift for my own twin sister, and I decide to get a similar papyrus for myself as well. This is a ritual of ours, to purchase two of what we truly love, in order to share with each other. These are never commercial souvenirs, but rare treasures found few and far between. Now a papyrus depicting loving twins will join the matching black pearl pendants she sourced from the Marshall Islands, and the emerald rings I found for us in Brazil.

To purchase a papyrus, you give the number under the artwork to one of the many roving salespeople, who write it on a paper pad, then rip it off and hand it to you. When ready, one submits the ticket to the tall counter at the back of the establishment, where payments are processed and neatly rolled papyrus in cardboard cylinders are dispensed.

Sara and I have snagged a salesperson, which is lucky because a buying frenzy of sorts has erupted in the gallery. I have my credit card out but the wide fulfillment counter is three people deep with customers handing up their paper orders and credit cards as if on the floor of a papyrus stock exchange. Sara is leading our scribe around the salon, pointing out her choices. She really enjoys shopping and the large amount of money she's recently inherited has provided some well-deserved discretionary funds. She's generous as well. It was Sara who secretly upgraded our red-eye plane tickets from Frankfurt to Cairo into First Class private sleeping pods. Priceless.

It's going to be awhile before Sara returns with her clerk or another salesperson frees up and I find myself standing alone holding my bank card. That's when I see Michael on the other side of the store, being chatted up by one of the women, Alicia, who is often found chatting him up. Alicia's gentle husband stands patiently by as she asks question after question. I don't blame her. Michael's absolutely charming, in addition to being a world expert on sacred sites and ancient spirituality. Alicia radiates a warm, matronly friendliness, but she can also seem intense. Right now, she appears to be in serious sponge mode, just soaking up the wisdom while she can, with him physically here. It *is* much more fun talking with someone in person compared to reading their books.

Michael is very tall and he's leaning down ever so slightly, head cocked, listening to Alicia. Our eyes lock and smile, and an impulse travels the photon highway between us.

I walk over and wave my bank card playfully in his face, which just happens to be a Star Wars branded Visa with a big black image of Darth Vader brandishing his light saber.

"I have no idea why you think I'm on the dark path," I tease.

"Give me that!" he snatches the card from my hand, holding it just out of my reach like a schoolboy flirting on the playground. "I want one of these."

Laughter and brief explanations ensue, which only a devout Star Wars fan would appreciate. Alicia is not that. She's standing silently; not even a chuckle about my Vader joke. Her unspoken irritation is palpable and I quickly decide to un-hijack the conversation.

"Ok, I have to go buy some papyrus," I plead, "I need my card."

Michael hands it back with a smile.

Eventually I find an employee to record my artwork identification numbers and I make my way to the counter to queue up, clutching my hand-scrawled order. The line is still long, giving me time to reflect. My thoughts drift to the challenges facing us twenty-first century spiritual seekers.

How insidious the temptation to indulge in the glamour of spiritual self-importance, or even drift into outright delusion. Yet once our internal code-reading apparatus is activated, we can no longer pretend we don't know exactly who and what we are encountering. I imagine a true Sorceress, upon finally wielding her sword of light, would be humbled and awed by the infinite landscape it illuminates stretching out before her. Then what is there to do but laugh? And play.

In her book *The Passion of Isis And Osiris*, Jean Houston speaks about the result of true initiation:

"The individual would know the initiation had taken root within the self when he saw the ordinary life had become extraordinary. It would simply be impossible for an initiate into the Mysteries to live his life as he had always lived, for the door between the worlds had blown apart...the initiate's consciousness had changed, and so to, his life ever after."

In other words, we can tell if we have integrated the teachings by simply looking at our lives. Are we tending to the same old aches and pains? Making sacrifices at the altar of ancient heartaches? Pruning our telomeres with the same old limiting stories? If we always have something to say, we give up the silent space to discover what we don't know we don't know. If we become addicted to the high of being admired and esteemed, we must be prepared for the other side of the coin: the empty desperation of relentlessly seeking others' validation.

I am reminded of a passage in the *Tao Te Ching*:

Be like the Tao
It can't be approached or withdrawn from,
benefited or harmed,
honored or brought into disgrace.
It gives itself up continually.
That is why it endures.[31]

---

[31] Mitchell, Stephen (translator). 2006. *Tao Te Ching: A New English Version* Harper Perennial Modern Classics, NY. (originally written by Lao Tzu)

"Here you go," the man behind the counter slides my receipt, bank card, and two cardboard cylinders of goddesses toward me. The containers are printed with a cluttered, touristy montage of mummies, pyramids and Nefertitis, but they will protect the precious contents when packing.

"Shukren," I reply, returning Vader to my pocketbook.

Walking out of the papyrus store, my heart feels soft and warm, like my darkness has fallen hopelessly in love with my light. My strength and weakness have embraced, birthing compassion. My goddess has accepted my god. I am, in this moment, exactly who and where I am supposed to be.

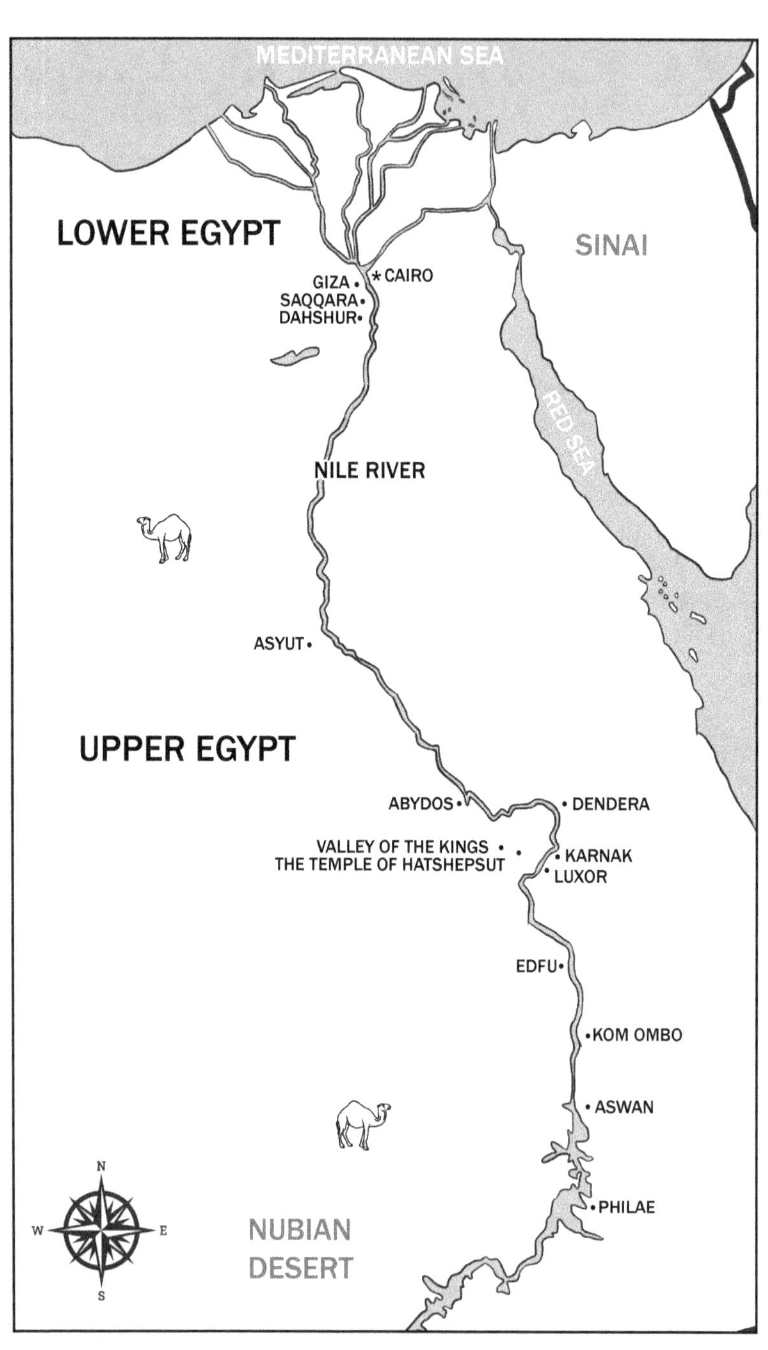

MEDITERRANEAN SEA
LOWER EGYPT
SINAI
GIZA
SAQQARA
DAHSHUR
CAIRO
RED SEA
NILE RIVER
ASYUT
UPPER EGYPT
ABYDOS
DENDERA
VALLEY OF THE KINGS
THE TEMPLE OF HATSHEPSUT
KARNAK
LUXOR
EDFU
KOM OMBO
ASWAN
PHILAE
N
W
E
S
NUBIAN
DESERT

Chapter 25

THE TEMPLE OF ISIS

The Temple of Isis, also known as Philae Temple, is on Agilika Island in the Nile river. But this wasn't always so. Philae Temple originally stood nearby on the now submerged island of Philae. In the sixties, UNESCO partnered with Egypt to relocate the temple stone by stone to Agilika Island. This was necessary because the 1902 construction of the low Aswan dam inundated the temple with water. By 1960, when the modern Aswan High Dam was engineered, a full third of the temple was submerged. Even today, visitors can see the discolored water line the temple wears as a result of this flooded period. Fearing the temple would be completely lost to the rising waters of Lake Nassar, a project began to save the structure. After building a cofferdam and temporarily pumping out the water around the monument, it was deconstructed into 40,000 individual components which were numbered, transported, and then reconstructed on nearby Agilika Island.

What the UNESCO/Egyptian restoration failed to take into account (or perhaps knew but proceeded anyway) was that the location itself was sacred.

Though the Temple of Isis was built in Ptolemaic times (690 CE) its prior location on Philae Island was one of the original, sacrosanct sites selected by the ancient gods themselves. "It appears that all major temple complexes are built on or beside primordial mounds…The sites of the historical temples at Edfu, Kom Ombo, Philae, Dendera, Karnak, and Luxor are each identified as a Great Seat of the First Occasion. This was an epoch when the primordial mounds were established along the course of the Nile to serve as foundations for future temples."[34]

Venerated since antiquity, these primordial mounds are often the intersection of electromagnetic and telluric forces that are believed to contribute to visitors' extrasensory experiences. When the Philae temple was moved, its physical body was relocated, but its energy body—it's spiritual technology—was left behind.

I don't want to be left behind on today's excursion to

---

[34]Silva, Freddy. 2012. *The Divine Blueprint Temples, Power Places, And The Global Plan to Shape the Human Soul.* Invisible Temple, Portland, ME, p. 63.

The Temple of Isis was flooded by the construction of the Aswan Dam. It was later moved, stone by stone, from Philae Island to Agilika Island.

the Temple of Isis, so I hurry down our riverboat's gangplank toward a smaller dock to the north. This is where we will depart for Agilika Island and I have about 15 minutes to catch the river taxi's pre-dawn departure.

Reaching the small dock, I step over the Nile's mythic waters and into a small, open-air boat about twenty feet long. The craft's roof is supported by intermittent posts, but it has no walls. Similar water taxis are used in the Amazon and Indonesia, and undoubtedly countless other places as well. For a passionate adventuress like myself, stepping down into a gently rocking boat and taking a seat on a wooden bench feels like sliding into a pew at church. Am I the only one who thinks the organic smell of a river blended with the low growl of an aft motor and cool splashes of water off the hull is as nostalgic as a favorite holiday dish?

Ra rises slowly, turning the river's black waters to orange and then to blue before we reach the first cataract of the Nile. I am enchanted. This rapid may have been formidable once, but I live in an area of the Pacific Northwest where snow-melt rivers rage every spring over head-cracking rocks and submerged logs, so these bubbling riffles with their darting swallows seem downright tranquil. Amongst the granite rock islands and deep green reeds, placid pools offer a blinding reflection of the intense Nubian sun. We motor pass shorelines of biblical description and the hotel where Agatha Christie lived while writing *Death on the Nile.*

Sliding up to the island dock that serves Philae temple tourists I can already see spectacular pillars, a majestic pylon, and an exotic wall all made of limestone. The location seems like something out of a dream. It seems as if the temple takes up almost the entire island! We bump up against the dock and the butterfly breeze kisses generated by our moving vessel condense into a hot cloak that wraps my body. The weather would be bearable if not delightful in a filmy sundress or light tank top, but in the conservative Nubian desert, my full-length cotton pants and sleeved shirt are all but required. Western women do get a pass of sorts however: my head is unveiled and my long hair tied up off my neck as I climb out of the water taxi and onto the small Agilika Island dock.

It's not time to tour the temple quite yet, however. Our first stop is a quaint alfresco eatery overlooking the Nile, shaded by a thatched roof and a collection of sun-bleached, Nestlé-branded café umbrellas. A wild-roaming domestic cat strolls with us to the stone tables, where we have been invited to eat our box lunches before visiting the temple.

Choosing our seats, we unburden ourselves of backpacks, hats, and cameras. Soon waiters arrive to offer bottled water and iced tea for sale.

"Bottled water please." I have barely made my request when the swarm arrives, rushing like a high tide along the cement floors, flowing in living rivers between the tables and against our legs.

An invasion of feral cats is streaming into the restaurant! Felines of every size, color, and coat pattern introduce themselves with squeaky-door squeals and raspy meows. Elegant females worthy of worship curl through the table legs while burly intact tomcats stand at our feet, demanding to be fed. Scattered throughout the congregation are a sprinkling of precious multi-colored kittens running with tiny tails pointed skyward.

The table beggars are being rewarded with bits of sandwich meat and pinches of bread which they gulp down gratefully. Despite a few cross snarls and paw swats, the multitudes seem peaceful. I'm relieved to see most of the cats look fairly well nourished. Some are affectionate, welcoming the gentle stroking and scratching offered by the cat lovers in the group. Other animals are truly feral, hovering just out of reach. They will run to consume a tossed treat but skitter away if approached.

I'm still waiting for my water when I notice a tiny creature wobbling in the walkway between the tables, about ten feet away. Making my way through the café and trying not to step on any cats, I reach down and scoop up the teeny white mammal. I return to my table cupping the little ball of silky fur, soft flesh, and fragile matchstick bones against my chest. The kitten is neither overfed nor alarmingly thin, but has the lean physique of a wild creature nurtured to nature's razor thin equation for optimum return on maternal investment. It peers up at me with glossy round eyes and the angular face of a classic Egyptian cat. The kitten is completely white except for a wrap of black across the forehead from which a nearly perfect inverted white triangle descends. I don't think this baby is weaned yet and have no intention of trying to feed it any solid food, but it's impossible to tell which milk-filled mother cat it belongs to. After a few more minutes of cuddling, I return the infant feline to where I found it, lowering it's weightless little body back to the cement walkway where four micro paws stand confidently for a few moments before sauntering away. In moments the nascent kitten disappears into the writhing maze of cats.

✳✳✳

Walking over the sandy, yellow-blonde isthmus that connects the cat café to the temple proper is a blistering hot proposition. I'm being hugged by the kind of humidity that can only be produced by triple–degree temperatures baking a landmass surrounded on all sides by water. Having been released to wander inside the temple, I bask in the beautiful energy left over from centuries of venerating the Divine Feminine. But it's indescribably hot, so when a gigantic stone doorway offers its shaded threshold, I happily slip inside. The ingress leads to an ancient, concealed passageway, shadowed, and cooler. Mystery clings to the massive masonry, as palpable as the damp tee shirt clinging to the butterflies in my belly. Curiosity takes me by the hand, pulling me forward, tempting me with the magic left behind by those who walked these stones long, long ago. Padding silently forward, unexpectedly isolated from the throng of tourists, I'm unsure of who—or what—I might meet around the next turn. I'm half expecting a shimmering Darth Vader to step out from behind the next stone!

A few steps further a sublime breeze ruffles my hair, chilling the perspiration on the back of my neck, and the megalithic tunnel opens to the river, revealing what was once a magnificent limestone terrace. Below, the sun-spangled blue waters of the Nile dance beguilingly around smitten granite boulders in an eternal romance. Time softens, as if I have just emerged from a limestone wormhole and I struggle to place myself accurately along its rapidly dissolving chronology. It is here, somewhere along this reed-choked Egyptian shoreline that baby Moses is supposed to have been found. But my interest stretches back even before biblical times. I am standing on this small island, in the Temple of Isis, as a modern day initiate, seeking the wisdom of the goddess.

Isis appeared in Egypt after the great flood, and, along with her husband and brother Osiris, began resurrecting the niceties of civilization: Agriculture, animal husbandry, herbal healing, marriage, weaving, and child rearing. That's not all Isis resurrected. In addition to being a compassionate mother figure to all humanity, Isis was an accomplished Sorceress. She is said to have been taught the words of magic by Thoth himself. Isis mastered shape-shifting, uttered spells with perfection, and was clever enough to trick Ra into revealing his *Ren* (Sacred Name). When Osiris was murdered by their brother Set, Isis took the form of a kite, and revived her husband long enough to conceive a son, Horus.

Each year, the Temple of Isis hosted a festival where the passion play of Isis and Osiris was performed in all its tragic detail. Local villagers participated in the drama and a lavish feast was prepared. Though the temple was inclusive, instruction in the high magic of Egyptian sexual alchemy and the ritual of living resurrection was reserved for devoted initiates of the temple who had proven themselves worthy through a long apprenticeship. Mary Magdalene may have studied here before meeting the magi Yeshua bin Joseph, who most westerners know as Jesus.

This is not what most of us were taught in Sunday School! By culling and rewriting the holy texts to reflect their agenda and torturing and murdering anyone who dared disagree, the so-called Holy Fathers waged the ultimate smear campaign. Mary Magdalene was branded a prostitute, and the story of the Garden of Eden was edited to place the blame squarely on Eve and the Serpent. Incidentally, the title of Serpent was historically reserved for the most spiritual, knowledgeable, and wise. Druids were known as "serpents" and these were likely the "snakes" Saint Patrick cast out of

Ireland. Although modern medicine still uses the caduceus as a logo—an homage to serpents' former symbolism—snakes and female sexuality are still vehemently reviled and feared by many.

Before the Caesars and Popes took control of our bodies and souls, the traditions and practices of the Old Religion included strengthening the light body, an 'etheric double' the Egyptians called the Ka. With the Ka sufficiently charged, a masterful Egyptian magi might demonstrate an enhanced ability to magnetize to herself or himself desired objects and events, or demonstrate powers of healing, levitation, and bi-location.

Tricia Mccannon, in her book *The Lost Years of Jesus*, has uncovered evidence that as a young man, Jeshua studied in the courts of Egypt, likely undertaking the years-long training required to use heka, the multilayered Egyptian magic of incantation, will, and pure intention. As unbelievable as it may sound to us today, heka allowed adepts to bend the laws of matter, to effect "miracles."

Another biblical character raised in Pharaoh's household, Moses, seems to have mastered similar feats of heka. Author Jean Houston explains, "...the mysteries of Ra taught the conscious art of manipulation of forms. Such high magic was said to allow the pharaoh to manifest the unmanifest, to command wind, water, and earth. At its lower level, it was throwing a staff to the ground and watching it change into a serpent."[35]

---

[35]Houston, Jean. 1995. *The Passion of Isis and Osiris.* Ballantine/ Wellspring (Random House), NY, p. 197.

Though impressive, these powers—which eastern yogic traditions call the Siddhis—were not the ultimate goal of the initiate. Misuse of the Siddhis might derail a lifetime of devoted practice and risk the displeasure of Ma'at in the underworld. The Egyptian goddess Ma'at, weighed the heart of the deceased at the portal to the Duat. If the heart was heavier than a feather, the petitioner was denied immortality. You see, the true purpose of the Egyptian mysteries was nothing less than eternal life.

Standing alone on a sun-baked limestone terrace, my feet on the very blocks from the Temple of Isis, I recommit myself to the Goddess. Here, in this temple, it seems possible to resurrect the golden age of Egypt, if only in my own heart and home. Soon I will reunite with my own Osiris. Not necessarily with a man (although that would be wonderful) but with the neter of Osiris inside me. Inter-twining the male and female within oneself and creating a complete spiritual being is a crucial goal for any aspiring modern Magi.

Now it's time to leave the Temple of Isis and I can't help but wonder: who is she really? Was she a flesh and blood woman? A cosmic consciousness preserved in myth? An extraterrestrial? In *The Golden Ass*, The Greek allegorist Apuleius allegedly quotes Isis herself:

"I who am Nature, the parent of things, the queen of all the elements, the primordial progeny of ages, the supreme of Divinities, the sovereign of the spirits of the dead, the first of the celestials, and the uni-form resemblance of gods and goddesses. I, who rule by my nod the luminous summits of the heavens, the salubrious breezes of the sea, the deplorable silences of the realms beneath, and whose one divinity the whole orb of earth venerates...Hence the primogenial

Phrygians call me Pessinuntica, the mother of the Gods; the Attic Aborigines, Cecropian Minerva; the floating Cyprians, Paphian Venus; the arrow-bearing Cretans, Diana Dictynna; the three-tongued Sicilians, Stygian Proserpine; and the Eleusinians, the Ancient Goddess Ceres. Some also call me Juno, others Bellona, others Hecate and others Rhamnusia. And those who are illuminated by the incipient rays of that divinity the Sun when he rises, the Ethiopians, the Arii, the Egyptians skilled in ancient learning, worship me by ceremonies perfectly appropriate and call me by my true name, Queen Isis."[36]

---

[36]Apulieus. 2nd century C.E. *The Golden Ass.* Book 11.

PART III:

THE
GREAT PYRAMID

Photo by Hossan M. Omar courtesy of Unsplash

Chapter 26

THE HOUSE OF OSIRIS

The sand under my hands and knees is soft and forgiving as I crawl forward on all fours but the small leather backpack I'm wearing keeps scraping on the ceiling of the two-and-a-half foot tall bedrock tunnel. There is no light in here, but my sight has adjusted just enough so that every now and then I turn my head to examine the intimately close rough-hewn sides of this, the deepest shaft of the Great Pyramid. Up ahead, at last, a small glowing square appears— the opening to the illuminated subterranean chamber. Crawling the last few yards, I try not to think about the fact that I'm deep underground and 2 ½ million stone blocks are stacked above my soft flesh, each block weighing about 2 tons. Reaching the opening and twisting out like a birthing baby, I clamber to my feet, brushing the sand of ages off my pants.

I'm somewhat disappointed. This purportedly sacred underground chamber is dusty, unfinished, and humid—a cave really. In the center is a seemingly bottomless dry well shaft encircled by what looks to be a pretty rickety, rusted rail fence, the kind one might find on the porch of an abandoned mobile home. Comfortingly, the central abyss has been filled in with decades of debris, so should the gaunt banister give way—or a reckless person tumble over—they would eventually hit bottom. The discovery of this rough grotto and its vertical chasm validated the account of the 5th century Greek historian Herodotus, who maintained it was connected to an even deeper chamber beneath the pyramid, complete with a small lake that once connected to the Nile River.

The Great Pyramid is certainly the most ancient initiation site available to the average tourist, and maybe this is as it should be. Nevertheless, I'm blessed to be here as part of a small group of spiritual pilgrims who have been granted private night-time access, thanks to our well-known tour guide and god knows how much baksheesh. And so, those among us who dared have elected to pattern our visit after the mystery traditions of old which dictate the initiate start at the lowest, roughest, most raw areas of the pyramid. Mimicking the architecture, we will progress upward through the House of Osiris, advancing through shafts, galleries, and chambers of evolving refinement. The intent is for our consciousness to do the same. Exploring the underground chamber, I steady myself with a hand on a conveniently placed boulder and wonder how many invisible handprints lie under my palm?

Though Herodotus implied that initiates ascended this area through an opening in the ceiling, at present there is no other way in or out except the claustrophobic rock tube that brought us here, so our group dutifully reverses course and disappears like a family of meerkats back into the stone.

After navigating a series of narrow rock shafts and scaling the iron ladders installed in modern times to connect them, one emerges into the 151 foot long Grand Gallery of the Great Pyramid. Stepping out onto one of the low stone ramps which run along both sides of the Gallery I can hardly believe my eyes. I have never been inside a gothic cathedral but I imagine this is how it must feel. High above the soaring stone walls, an elegant, nearly thirty-foot tall corbelled ceiling crowns the Grand Gallery, which itself slants upward toward the renowned King's Chamber. Recently, a team of French and Japanese scientists using Muography—a form of surveying using particle physics—discovered a previously unknown "void" in the space above the Grand Gallery. It seems that above this remarkable ceiling, an additional room of similar proportions exists, one that no human has ever seen—at least for thousands of years.

Some of the oldest quoted historians like the Arabian writer Ibn Abd Alhokm maintain that the Giza pyramids were constructed as a repository for "talismans...and strange things...and riches and treasures, and signatures made of precious stones..." This was undertaken because the King of Egypt had a vision in which he saw the land and the people destroyed by a cataclysm of fireballs and a relentless deluge. The King, Saurid Ibn Salhouk, who is said to have lived 300 years before the flood, set about preserving "the commentaries of the Priests in chests of black marble...in which were the wonders of his profession, and of his actions, and of his nature, and what was done in his time, and what is, and what shall be, from the beginning of time to the end of it."[37]

Other items purportedly stashed away inside the treasuries of the pyramid include metal which does not rust, glass which bends but doesn't break, strange spells, *akakirs* (aromatic roots), and deadly poisons. Even more obscure stories maintain that a room meeting the description of the newly discovered void contains a "chair" made of a yet unknown iron-type metal that Osiris used to travel to the constellation Orion!

Today, lighting installed along the walls of the Grand Gallery illuminates one's way as s/he ascends the ancient cathedral deep inside the pyramid. At the top of the Grand Gallery and through a megalithic granite anteroom one arrives at the final passageway to the Kings Chamber of the Great Pyramid. On the left wall, a half-height stone doorway and equally low dark tunnel require every visitor to bend forward and walk the last eight feet of the entry access in a physically induced supplication of sorts. Why the most intriguing areas of many Egyptian monuments must be entered through impractically small stone apertures is a fact up for debate. It may be a reminder for initiates to remain humble to the end, a forced bow if you will, as they enter the most Holy of Holies.

---

[37]Greaves, John. 1646. *The Enduring Mystery, Pyramidographia.*

Chapter 27

THE KING'S CHAMBER

It was nighttime as we stooped our way through the final musty passageway deep within the Great Pyramid and entered the famous King's Chamber. Once in, I stand upright and walk a few steps forward, finding myself in a massive rectangular room made of rock. Modeling some others in the group, I take off my shoes and socks and place them along the wall near the door. The chamber measures 34.4 ft. from east to west and 17.17 ft. north to south.[38] At the far end,

---

[38]The King's Chamber measures 20 Egyptian Royal cubits or 10.47 metres (34.4 ft) from east to west and 10 cubits or 5.234 metres (17.17 ft) north to south. It has a flat roof 11 cubits and 5 digits or 5.852 metres (19 feet 2 inch) above the floor.

away from the entry, stands the imposing sarcophagus, open and empty. Despite what most of us were taught—that this was the burial chamber of Pharaoh Cheops—no body or mummy has ever been found interred here, or in any of the eight great Egyptian pyramids. Even to the casual observer, it's obvious that this ginormous stone box would never have fit through the small entryway. Somehow, the structure was built around it.

The glow from electric lights installed in modern times around the perimeter of the floor ushers my eyes up the nineteen-plus feet of red granite walls toward the room's roof where nine impossibly large stone slabs form a perfectly flat ceiling. And then I feel the pulsing. Is it the interior space of the King's Chamber, me, or the pyramid itself vibrating? It's impossible to tell. I no longer have a credible sense of these boundaries, which moments ago seemed obvious. And I don't care! I am immersed in the energetic thrumming of the place. The intensity seems to enter through my chest, strong but not uncomfortable. I feel what can only be described as a gentle pressure acting upon and within every cell of my body. It takes considerable effort to refocus my attention on Michael as he arranges our group in a circle. I'm enchanted, feeling buoyant, weightless, and physically supported by the resonance of the place.

And then Michael has the guards turn off all the lights.

With ancient sounds held sacred for thousands of years, our group begins toning. It is utterly pitch black. I can't see anyone or anything in the room, not even my hand when I lift it in front of my face. In this moment we exist as a group of invisible spirits, manifest only by our individual melodies.

The chamber's acoustics receive our sonant voices, the walls modulating them into a single cosmic song that reverberates potently around the chamber. Beneath my feet, the floor starts rocking and rolling like a ship in high seas.

This is the same sensation I experienced in the chapel at Dendera, but way more extreme. And in the dark it is significantly more disorienting. Nevertheless, I feel extremely lucid, fully embodied, and acutely aware of the incredulous feel of the megalithic stone floor dropping away under my heels. I lose my balance and stumble forward. Someone catches me—it's too dark to see who—and pulls me to my feet but I continue to wobble. It's difficult to find places on the floor where the stone is still solid enough to stand on. By now my eyesight has adjusted enough to see shadows and intuit my fellow travelers in the room. I don't sense anyone else falling down or through the floor, so I decide to focus on joining the guided meditation in progress.

We are being invited to close our eyes and experience ourselves as our true nature—as stars traveling along the great serpent in the sky, the Milky Way.

We are to imagine a time before we came to this planet, and it is suggested we allow ourselves to flow along in this river of stars until a tributary appears that beckons us. To the right or to the left, or downward, our path will appear, and we may see our soul's descent into matter, on this planet or perhaps another. We will know from whence we came, and perhaps why we are here.

Focusing my inner vision with the sincerest of intent, I float along in my mind's eye, in a warm dark ocean punctuated by luminous, spinning galaxies. Oh no! I am clearly too far out in the cosmos, and I have totally lost sight of which river of stars I'm supposed to be following. Like a surfer who has inadvertently paddled out far beyond where the waves are breaking, I need to get my shamanic journeying back inside. Then I hear a voice. It is close and clear but it has that unique clairaudient quality I've experienced before. I suspect no one else hears it.

"Look up."

In the few moments it takes to open my eyes and reorient myself in relation to the red granite walls, I realize the floor has stabilized under my feet. I take a few steps forward and look up. Where the megalithic flat granite roof used to be there is a large clear tube extending through the top of the pyramid and out into space. The most delicate light is streaming down through the portal, faintly blue, and breathtakingly beautiful. On high, the channel is literally awash with an ethereal luminosity. Small glowing orbs are elegantly spiraling down like effulgent celestial streamers. Shocked, enchanted, and frankly in disbelief, I close my eyes to clear what must be my overactive imagination. After a bit of psychological and physical grounding, I peek up again. It's still there!

Incredulous, I walk in the darkness toward the portal and gaze up to take in the scope of the supernal phenomenon. Its incandescent mist, still falling, bathes me in a hermetical spotlight. Despite being totally encharmed, my inner scientist demands more focused observation. I note that, just outside the effects of the dimensional rift, I can clearly see the individual rough stone blocks of the pyramid's interior structure, stacked upon each other and rising upward to the apex. Far, far above, at the very top, familiar stars twinkle faintly in the blue-black sky. Again, a wave of skepticism washes over me, and I close my eyes, reaffirming to myself my waking, sober state. I took no drugs, hallucinogens, or plant medicines before entering the monument. When I open my eyes a third time and find the portal still there, my skepticism dissolves into pure wonder. I imagine I look like one of the girls from Fatima, wandering slowly with my head angled up toward the heavens.

After I don't know how long, I notice the people in our group taking turns lying in the almost four-ton sarcophagus. I wait silently in line and when it is my turn to climb in, I do so without hesitation. The walls of the granite box are actually pretty tall, so a shorter person like myself has to attempt a maneuver similar to a gymnast mounting a balance beam and then swinging a leg over to enter the space. In a most surreal action, I lay down on my back in the Egyptian sarcophagus. The lid is long gone, so no worries of being truly entombed, but it is surprisingly deep. Some people have experienced out of body journeys while in repose here but for me the feeling is intensely relaxing. I find myself stroking the walls of the sarcophagus, which seem to tenderly hug my shoulders. I examine the speckled pink pattern of the granite and the polished workmanship of the interior, still evident after thousands of years. Weirdly, it isn't dark or the least bit unnerving; in fact it feels quite cozy. Almost slightly sedating. Laying flat on my back, I can really take in the sight of the portal, which still suffuses the roof of the chamber with spectacular lucency. I am completely sober and self-aware and have accepted the astonishing fact that an interdimensional opening has manifested in the King's chamber, rising through the apex of the pyramid and extending out into space! I could stay here forever, held by the loving granite arms of the sarcophagus and staring, transfixed, at the otherworldly miracle of the portal. It feels like I am alone inside a dark, magical world, but also, I know I am part of a tour group inside the Great Pyramid. I inhabit these two realities with ease. In the second reality—and knowing the 'pyramid etiquette,'—I clamber back out of the sarcophagus to make room for the next guest.

One by one, we each take a turn lying in the so-called funerary box. I do not believe we were lying in a crypt. The most prominent Pharaohs—including King Tutankhamen— were buried miles to the south in the Valley of the Kings. When archaeologists first penetrated the step pyramid at Saqqara, for example, its entrance was still sealed, the virginal alabaster sarcophagus untouched by burglars or tomb robbers. Upon opening it, there was nothing inside.

John Anthony West, in his scholarly reinterpretation of an even earlier thesis by Egyptologist Schwaller de Lubicz, writes, "In support of this theory [the pyramids being tombs] there is no direct or indirect evidence whatsoever. While the numerous small pyramids of Middle and Late Kingdom Egypt were clearly and obviously designed as tombs, and have disclosed a wealth of mummies and coffins, the eight 'great' pyramids of the Old Kingdom have revealed no sign of either coffin or mummy. The construction of these vast edifices differs in every way from the later tombs. The curious, slanting passageways could not possibly be less conducive to the elaborate funerary rituals for which Egypt was famed. The stark interiors of the 'tomb chambers' stand in vivid contrast to the lavishly inscribed and carved chambers of later Egypt."[39]

---

[39]West, John Anthony. 1993. *Serpent in the Sky The High Wisdom of Ancient Egypt.* Quest Books, Theosophical Publishing House, IL, p. 13.

Ancient mystery traditions the world over describe sacred initiations in which a living human is given a glimpse of the otherworld, then resurrected to live out their lives as enlightened path-showers, sometimes exhibiting enhanced psychic or clairvoyant skills. These rituals were undertaken at night, in a sensory-deprived environment, like a cave, underground grotto, or stone receptacle. Weekend warriors need not apply, for years of study were required and even then, some initiates actually died or went mad. The men and women that lived to see the morning star were deemed "risen."

My experience in the King's Chamber makes me wonder if the granite sarcophagi act like an anesthesia of sorts, assisting the prepared human into an altered state, or even a kind of suspended animation. In such a state, released from physical needs or distractions, the information stored in the quartz-laden room, or even other dimensions, might be accessed. If these really are 'living resurrection' devices, perhaps the hidden caves, protective dolmens, and granite boxes deep inside pyramids are somehow designed to shield the initiates' physical form from intrusive energies while the spirit is on walkabout.

One point all ancient mystery traditions agree on is this: Union with the Sacred Feminine, the Divine Sophia, is the key to the Kingdom.

Despite the masculine red-granite it is composed of, the King's Chamber, as a place of spiritual initiation, requires the metaphysical consent of a Goddess for it to work. For those who have wedded the priest and priestess within themselves, the energies of Isis and Osiris can combine inside this sacred bedchamber—and inside the sacred human—

and create the High God Horus. When Horus takes flight, a human is "transformed into a god, into a bright star."

I don't know how much time passed before our own modern high priest emerged from his turn in the sarcophagus, alighting from his flight to gather us once again. With magical incantations Michael collects our tribe together. In what feels like a waking dream, I back myself against a wall of the King's Chamber, needing to make visceral contact with the stone. In a moment of material mindfulness, I place my palms against the enormous granite block supporting me, becoming present to its truly mysterious past.

Before I journeyed to Giza, I had read accounts of white-robed priests emerging out of these hallowed stones so at this point, I wasn't exactly shocked to see just such entities across the room, materializing in a line behind Michael. Unlike the portal, which continues to appear in clear focus, the monks present as nebulous apparitions that never fully resolve into the dimension I am occupying. Their long white robes emit a very subtle sheen but every time I try to look at their faces, they phase slightly out of focus. Above, the portal still shines, but its luminosity does not reach the inky depths of the chamber perimeter where I am standing. Like a child playing hide and seek in the dark, I sense a shadow standing beside me. It is Alicia. I turn, reaching my arm out to gently touch her shoulder in an 'Are you seeing this?' gesture and watch my hand fall right through a translucent human. This is *not* Alicia; it isn't even a physical person!

And then they are everywhere. The King's Chamber is chock full of these see-through people. They do not react or interact with me. I inspect a nearby man; I am so close I can see the stitching on his safari-style shirt and his clean shaven face. I am literally inches away but he stares straight ahead, seemingly unaware of my presence. He feels neither friendly nor threatening. Am I seeing imprints of people who have been here in the past—or will be here in the future? Am I the ghost here? I stand silently among an implausible crowd of transparent people, twelve or so priestly apparitions, and twenty-five flesh and blood humans.

What happened next was personal, powerful, and probably best kept as a private memory, though memory is a faded word to describe the experience. I can say that I had been studying the Emerald Tablets and felt well prepared for the adventure and unafraid of the dark. The gift I received is something I'm still integrating. If you think the previous tale is hard to believe, you'd think I'm truly crackers if I tried to describe the rest.

There is an old story of dubious origin about Napoleon spending the night inside the King's Chamber. When they let him out the next day he ran from the pyramid, white as a sheet, and forbade anyone to ask him about his experience. On his deathbed, Napoleon finally agreed to share what had happened that night and then just shrugged and said, "What's the use, you'd never believe me." I think I understand how Napoleon must have felt!

I become aware of the group reforming once again, clasping hands, forming a ring. By now my eyes have adjusted quite well, and I am nearer the light of the portal. Yes, it is still there! I find myself on the left side of Michael, holding his hand. On his other side is beautiful Elle, whose soul energy and life accomplishments I greatly admire, but who I haven't gotten to know very well.

I turn toward them. "The people were here."

Michael leans down toward me, "Yes, lots of people."

"I saw the portal. I saw you leave. I didn't know if you were coming back."

Michael squeezes my hand and the lights flash back on in the King's Chamber, their photons returning the megalithic stone roof to its position above me. My fellow initiates murmur and mill about like nightclub patrons at closing time, collecting their things and finding their friends.

In a flush of spiritual sobriety, I have the undeniable urge to get the hell out of this pyramid! I don't even put my shoes back on before I skip down the impossibly tall Grand Gallery (there was no one else in there), climb down the metal ladder then crouch my way down and then up through the main shaft to the entrance. Halfway out, a husky uniformed guard takes pity on me, asking why my husband doesn't feed me enough. I just smile at him and scamper on; this is not the time to explain that being single and skinny isn't necessarily a bad thing in my culture. The first thing I see upon emerging out of the Great Pyramid and into the balmy night air are the twinkling yellow lights of Cairo. Then I look up at the stars.

Chapter 28

DRINKING STARS

Had the King's Chamber, perhaps a sort of pineal gland of the pyramid, acted on my own pineal gland to create a lucid, stable, and sustained vision of another reality? Was the King's Chamber designed to effect a DMT dump in the brains of initiates? Do the megalithic pink granite walls, floor, and ceiling of the King's Chamber create a space where the Earths' geomagnetic field is altered? Magnetism is known to affect the magnetite crystals in our brains as well as the iron in our blood. Under the right conditions, magnetic stimulation of the brain induces dreamlike states, even in waking consciousness.[41] In an environment where geomagnetic field intensity is decreased, people are known to experience psychic and shamanic states.[42] Or did I witness an actual inter-dimensional opening? Or a rip in time? Or all of the above? If the King's Chamber is a working portal, could it also act, under the right conditions and intentions, as a physical portal to literally beam human bodies to the star Orion as the ancient Egyptian texts claim?

Clearly, the pyramid can alter consciousness and create a state of enhanced awareness. It seems this altered sensory state may allow us to see vivid visions, past and future timelines, and even portals and gateways into other dimensions! While in this altered state, the monuments themselves may take on personalities and facilitate contact with the "gods."

But why did I experience this?

To answer this we must think like an ancient Egyptian and ask the heart. It is the heart who, in the halls of Amentet (the underworld) decides whether the deceased is worthy to join Osiris in eternal life. Perhaps the vibration of our

---

[41]Persinger, M.A., Ruttan, L.A., and Koren, S. 1990. *Enhancement of temporal lobe-related experiences during brief exposures to milligauss intensity ELF magnetic field.* Journal of Biochemistry, 9, p.p. 33-45. Becker, Robert and Seldon, Gary. 1985. *The Body Electric: Electromagnetism and the Foundation of Life.* Quill, William Morrow, NY. Dubrov, A.P. 1978. *The Geomagnetic Field and Life: Geo-magnetobiology.* Plenam Press, NY. Kirschvink, J.L. et al. 1992. *Magnetite biomineralization in the human brain.* Proceedings of the National Academy of Sciences, 89: 7683-7687

[42]Roney-Dougal, Serena. 2002. *The Faery Faith, Green Magic.* London, *p.p.10-14.* May, E.C. et al. 1988. Review of the psychoenergetic research conducted at SRI International. SRI International Technical Report

hearts, tuned by our deepest and truest emotions, beliefs, desires, and actions is the silent song that the temples hear. The resonance of our hearts is like a credit card chip that the temples can read, unlocking their mythical powers.

These puzzling ideas flew around my mind like a cast of falcons, twisting and turning—working together but never quite cooperating—as our tall bus descended the short distance from the Giza plateau to our hotel at the base of the pyramids.

With a long sigh from the pneumatic brakes, the bus comes to a stop, its heavy motor silenced for the last time on this charter. Holding my backpack to my chest, I grip the hand-rail as my cloth boot feels for the ground below the last extra-tall step. Behind me emerge the couples on the trip, including Kurt and his wife, and then the single ladies, including Grey Bob. One by one they twist down the steep bus steps with one hand on the pole.

Down hop the smiling, friendly Australians, always the life of the party. I remember the bottles of Obelisk brand Sauvignon Blanc we shared on the top deck of the ship one dark Egyptian night. I watch with wonder the young man whose neck is wrapped loosely with a Keffiyeh, his sun-tanned face sporting several days of roguish stubble. Could this Indiana Jones-ish fella be the same pale, bespectacled young man who shyly boarded the bus at the beginning of the trip?

I retreat from the fray, positioning myself off to the side of the lobby on a path at the top of some wide steps where I can watch the mass of humanity pooling under the freakishly bright lights of the hotel's port cochère. Apparently some people are leaving straight away to catch flights home. Others are transferring to a hotel at the Cairo airport in preparation for early morning departures. The execution of such logistics seems inconceivable in my present state and I'm thankful Sara and I have a leisurely morning at the hotel tomorrow. The fragrance of night blooming jasmine wafts from the foliage behind me as the two Aussie ladies levitate towards me in slow motion. Looking down, I discover their feet are, in fact, touching the ground. They'll be leaving for the airport shortly and we hug our goodbyes, causing the atmosphere to wobble ever so slightly as if I've almost re-entered reality. Then they are gone and I watch as Michael approaches, reaching for me.

"Darling," he greets me with our little inside joke, pulling me close. I think he expects the usual cheek-to-cheek air kisses but in my altered state I just go straight in. Microseconds before our lips touch he turns toward my cheek in a bumpy, touch-and-go type of kiss.

"Well, I really messed that up," he laughs.

I should be embarrassed. Or relieved. In Egypt, a public kiss between a man and a woman falls somewhere between uncouth and criminally prosecutable.

"Are you going to dinner in the restaurant?" he asks.

"Yes," I realize I haven't eaten since lunch and it's now late evening. Just then Sara appears with several other women eager to say goodbye to Michael.

"Let's go to the restaurant," I suggest to Sara, leaving Michael to the ladies.

"OK, do you want to go back to the room first or are you too hungry?" Sara knows I can't go too long without eating.

"Too hungry," I smile.

Without delay we walk down the pathway that leads from the hotel lobby to the lawn, then over a shallow water feature to the hotel's outdoor dining pavilion. A waiter shows us to a large table, even though it is just the two of us. Soon several others from our group arrive and ask to join us. Everyone seems giddy. Even Alicia's skeptical husband confesses he saw stars inside the pyramid. I keep quiet and order a cheeseburger and a bottle of champagne. Soon, the waiter pops and pours, dealing out the delicate fizzing flutes.

"To the King's Chamber!" We all toast and sip. The libation is dry, sparkling, and perfect, like the night.

I remember what the monk Dom Perignon exclaimed when he invented champagne.

"I am drinking stars!" I exclaim.

That's when I see Michael sitting at a table for two next to the reflecting pool. He is gesturing toward the open chair, inviting me to join him.

We have already been seated and served our drinks so I indicate to Michael that he should come to the larger table and take the chair next to mine, which he does. Having collected his things and settled in next to me, he proceeds to chat up the table in his usual extroverted fashion. Why didn't I take my glass and walk over to that table? I was just so shocked that I hesitated. Maybe it isn't time yet for me to share my experience, even with Michael. Maybe that's why I stayed in my seat.

And so the conversation floats superficially around the table while the alchemy of the night scintillates, unspoken, between Michael and I. Uninhibited by physical density or decorum, our ka bodies lean close across the wide arms of the chairs like old friends or new lovers. Just up the hill, the Great Pyramid is lit up for the night. I pour Michael a glass of champagne.

"Thank you," he smiles, taking a sip as the waiter places the dinner I ordered in front of me.

The smell of the food brings my famished stomach instantly to life. I am raising the juicy burger to my lips when Michael looks at his watch and pushes back his chair.

"I've got to go," he says, standing up. "My flight leaves early in the morning and I'm going to the airport hotel tonight. The bus leaves in a few minutes."

I drop my burger back on the plate as he takes a final nip of champagne before placing the stemware on the table.

He's leaving? My mind is struggling to grasp what is happening. I have been one-hundred percent in the moment since the King's Chamber. I haven't had a chance to think this through! I need to ask him about the people in the King's Chamber, to know if he saw the portal, to tell him a giant ethereal white falcon flew up from the sarcophagus as he lay inside. Now all I can do is watch as Michael cordially and casually says his goodbyes to everyone over the tabletop. At

last he is finished and turns to me, taking my hand as I sit in
my chair. I don't have any idea what he's saying. I seem to be
inhabiting two realities at once. Michael holds my hand for
a long time, or it may have been only moments. Gently, as if
in slow motion, he backs away, our arms stretching to keep
our hands clasped. Then, with the Great Pyramid watching,
Michael smiles and turns to go, our fingertips slipping apart.

Afwan

"You're welcome," in Egyptian Arabic (spelled phonetically)

Amdwat (Duat, Dwat)

The Egyptian underworld, or otherworld. A parallel dimension interpenetrating the physical world, yet eternal and without time as we know it. The realm from which physical forms are born and where they return when they die. The dead traveled through the halls of the Duat, meeting the gods of the underworld, seeking transfiguration. The Amdwat was not a theoretical place; it was considered as real as the physical world and accessible to the living. Initiates who traveled there and returned were transformed into an *Akh*, a spiritually illuminated, "resurrected" being.

Ankh

The Egyptian "cross" with the loop at the top is a symbol of eternal life.

Akh

The spiritual part of the soul, mysteriously linked in Egyptian religion to the circumpolar or "imperishable" stars. A living human being who had direct experience of the otherworld and returned illuminated was said to become an *Akh*, a "bright star."

Anpu/Wepawet/Upuaut

A jackal or wolf-headed guardian god of the dead or otherworld. Like the better known *Anubis*, Wepawet was considered the "opener of the way." Anpu embodied the winter solstice and southern way, whereas Anubis was the personification of the summer solstice and northern "roads." The city of Assiut/Asyut was Wepawet's cult center.

Anubis

Lord of the Dead. The god of mummification who accompanies the deceased into the hall of judgment for the "weighing of the heart ceremony." Traditionally pictured as a well-built man with the head of a black jackal or wolf. Anubis is a devout protector and guardian, also considered the god of intuition. Personification of the summer solstice,

Apis

The sacred bull considered to represent—or even house—the soul of the god Osiris. Young Apis bulls were selected by Egyptian priests trained to identify the peculiar markings indicative of their godly status. The bulls were housed and fed with the respect due a god, and upon death received honor and ceremony similar to a Pharaoh.

Aswan

A city in Upper Egypt, near the first cataract (rapids) of the Nile. A primary location for Egyptian trade with Nubia.

Ba

The divine, immortal soul. It has eternal powers and the ability to travel from earth to the heavens and back. The ba could assume any form it wished and was most often represented by the hieroglyph of a human–headed hawk.

Backsheesh

The phonetic pronunciation of the Egyptian Arabic word for tip, bribe, or gratuity.

Cast

A falconry term meaning multiple trained falcons that are flown at one time when hunting.

Deir el-Bahri

The mortuary complex where the temple of Hatshepsut—the queen who became Pharaoh—is located. It is on the west side of the Nile, on the opposite side of the mountain range from the Valley of the Kings.

Dehenet

A tall, pyramid–shaped mountain that rises above the Valley of the Kings in Egypt. Considered the embodiment of the goddess Hathor.

Dendera

The location of the Temple of Hathor in Upper Egypt, known to the Egyptians as *Iunet.* Every year the cult statue of goddess Hathor was ceremoniously sailed to Edfu for a conjugal visit with the statue of Horus at his temple there. The earliest known representation of the zodiac was found on the ceiling of the Dendera temple.

Decans

In astrology, a decan is the subdivision of a sign. In ancient Egyptian astronomy, the decans are 36 groups of stars used to conveniently divide the 360 degree ecliptic into 36 parts of 10 degrees each.

Djed

An ancient and mysterious symbol in Egyptian religion. It is a pillar-like shape with four crossbars believed to represent stability and/or the backbone of the resurrected god Osiris. Curiously, it is said that the djed was used to transfigure human flesh into a spiritual form in the underworld. The act of "raising the djed" is depicted on Egyptian temple walls and djed pillar amulets are common in Egypt even today. In the classically multi-layered meanings characteristic of Ancient Egypt, "raising the djed" was also an alchemical practice of directing life-force energy up the spine/chakras to the brain, eventually generating the *Uraeus.*

Djoser

King Djoser ruled Egypt during the Third Dynasty of the Old Kingdom (circa 2,650 BCE). Djoser is best known for building the Step Pyramid at Saqqara, which is constructed out of stone blocks rather than mud bricks, under the direction of the famed architect Imhotep.

Durative

Author Jean Houston describes the durative realm as the timeless, eternal realm in which all of history exists; the time/space continuum. The "place" where the akashic records exist.

Edfu

The cult center of the elder hawk-god Horus and the location of the Temple of Horus in Upper Egypt. On the map, Edfu is south of Thebes (Luxor/Karnak) and north of Aswan. Sacred writings found at Edfu temple describe medicine, ritual, astronomy, and how civilization was restarted after the great flood by creator gods who identified sacrosanct locations where future temples were to be built.

Fez

A brimless, cylindrical hat with a flat top that usually has a tassel. Worn traditionally by men in eastern Mediterranean countries.

Hathor/Ninmah

The Egyptian and Sumerian names respectively for the most ancient Egyptian sky-goddess, Creatrix of humankind, mother of humanity. It is from her Sumerian name Nin*mah* that our word Ma/Mama is derived. The beloved daughter of Ra and consort of Horus is said to have arrived in Egypt from a mysterious land to the south called Punt. She is often depicted as a woman with cow ears—or completely bovine. Hathor's headdress is a sun disk cradled by cow horns. Goddess of women, love, childbirth, dance, music, and drunkenness. Hathor is also associated with astrology, turquoise, and the art of sound healing. Her cult center/temple is located in Dendera, Egypt.

Heka

Egyptian magic. Words of power. The sacred names of the gods. Spells, magic prayers, and healing incantations were effective only if the proper words were spoken in a specific order, with correct intonation and proper intent. Heka required knowing not only the names of the gods, which were hidden, but the correct pronunciation, known only to the priest magician or priestess/sorceress.

Heliacal

Relating to or near the sun—used especially of the last setting of a star before and its first rising after invisibility due to conjunction with the sun

Hermetic/Hermetic Seal

1. Relating to the mystical and alchemical writings or teachings arising in the first three centuries BCE and attributed to Hermes Trismegistus ("Thrice Greatest Hermes") who is said to be the reincarnation of the Egyptian god Thoth.

2. An airtight, impervious seal (from the belief that Hermes Trismegistus invented a magic seal to keep vessels airtight).

Horus

The heroic hawk-headed, solar god. Son of Isis and Osiris, grandson of Thoth, who defeated his evil uncle Seth and reunited Upper and Lower Egypt. The symbolic harbinger of a golden age. Both an "elder" and "younger" form of Horus are known, one of whom was the lover of the goddess Hathor, who bore him a son.

Hypostyle

In architecture, a hypostyle hall or room has a roof which is supported by columns or rows of columns.

Imhotep

The renowned healer, scholar, and architect who built the stepped pyramid at Saqqara for King Djoser during the Third Dynasty (2,686-2,623 BCE). Imhotep was the only historical, non-royal person in Egypt to achieve the status of a god.

Isis

The goddess Isis is the embodiment of the Divine Feminine, a devoted benefactor of humanity, and the personification of the star Sirius (Sothis). Goddess of wisdom, cereals, healing, and magic, Isis was considered the ultimate sorceress, who was taught the words of power (heka) by Thoth himself. Using her magic, Isis was able to revivify her deceased husband Osiris long enough to conceive their son Horus. Isis can be identified in art by her throne (chair) headdress, symbolic of her Egyptian name *Auset*, which translates as "seat" or "throne." Her temple at Philae in Upper Egypt was the last place the mysteries of the Old Religion were taught—well into historical times—and may have been where Jesus spent his "lost years."

Jesses

The soft, flexible strips of leather attached to a trained falcon's legs. A falconer grasps or tethers the jesses to her glove, preventing the raptor from flying away.

Ka

A luminous, quantum-esque, etheric "double," or light body that every human possesses. This electromagnetic doppelgänger can, when sufficiently "charged" elevate one's consciousness, walk through walls, bi-locate, and even survive after the death of the physical body (khat).

Karnak

A temple complex—the largest known in the world—on the east bank of the Nile River which was part of ancient Thebes. Karnak is known for its staggeringly huge hypostyle hall, sprawling reflecting pool, and soaring obelisks. Site of the Alabaster Chapel and the White Chapel.

Keffiyeh

An Arab headdress consisting of a square of (usually patterned) cloth folded to form a triangle and held on by a cord, or simply wrapped like a scarf. Also known in Arabic as a ghutrah or shemagh.

Khat

The physical, flesh and blood, third–dimensional body that decays after death.

Kom Ombo

A temple on the Nile River in Upper Egypt north of Aswan. This unusual dual temple was built in Ptolemaic times (305 BCE–30 BCE), although, like most temples, there is evidence it sits on the site of an older sacred site. One side of the temple is dedicated to Horus, the solar hawk god, and the other to Sobek, "Lord of the Crocodiles."

Luxor

The modern name of the ancient city of Opet, where the Temple of Luxor is located. Part of ancient Thebes, the Luxor temple was historically linked to Karnak Temple by an avenue bordered with sphinxes. Cult center of the god Amun.

Monolith/Monolithic

A single large, unbroken piece of stone. Monolithic architecture is carved from one single massive rock (or bedrock) or is built using multi-ton stone blocks assembled together.

Neter/ Neteru

Singular and plural ancient Egyptian words for the

creator gods and goddesses. The spiritual life-force, intelligence, and consciousness present in all beings, matter, and phenomenon: from stones to angels, stars to storms.

Nubia

Ancient region in northeastern Africa, extending approximately from the Nile River valley (near the first cataract in Upper Egypt) eastward to the shores of the Red Sea, southward to what is now Sudan, and westward to the Libyan Desert.

Nut/Nuit

The primordial sky goddess, wife of the Earth (Geb) and mother of the sun (Ra) who she births every morning at dawn and swallows at dusk. The stars are said to be souls in her body whom she carries on her back in the Boat of Million Years, perhaps a euphemism for a starship?

Osiris

Beloved Egyptian god of resurrection, love, and sacrifice who helped restart human civilization after the great flood. His Egyptian name is *Ausir* or *Asar.* The son of Geb and Nut, husband of Isis, and father of Horus and Anubis. After he was murdered by his brother Seth, Osiris ruled the underworld and judged the souls of the newly deceased. Osiris is mysteriously linked to the djed pillar, the area around Abydos and the Great Pyramid of Giza, sometimes known as the "House of Osiris."

Philae

An island in the Nile River in Upper Egypt, south of the city of Aswan, where the temple of Isis was located. The last bastion of the Egyptian Mysteries and Old Religion. It is said that Isis awaited the annual resurrection of Osiris here (the inundation of the Nile) at which time she rose as the star Sothis (Sirius).

Pre-Diluvial

The time period in the Bible between the fall of man and the Genesis flood narrative. Corresponds to Earth's history prior to the Younger Dryas cataclysms which occurred at the end of the Pleistocene, approximately 12,800 years ago.

Precession (of the Equinoxes)

As the earth orbits counter-clockwise around the Sun, it also spins in a counter-clockwise direction itself. However the Earth's rotation has a slight "wobble." This axial tilt—called obliquity—causes the Sun (viewed on the equinoxes)to appear to rise against different constellations throughout the ages. It takes 72 years for just one degree of movement along the 360 degree circle of twelve constellations commonly known as the zodiac. A full cycle takes 25,920 years. Because many ancient temples and monuments were sited to specific constellations or stars, the year(s) during which those stars are "aligned" with the structure can help date the temple.

Ra

Egyptian sun god who is personification of sunlight and sustainer of life. Child of the sky goddess Nut, who births him at dawn and devours him at dusk. Ra's symbol is the phoenix, or *bennu* bird.

Saqqara

A village/region in the Giza area which contains a vast ancient necropolis (burial ground) as well as numerous pyramids and temples, including the Stepped Pyramid of Djoser, the Pyramid of Unas, and the Serapeum.

Sistrum

An ancient rattle-type instrument linked to the goddess Hathor, which may have been used for sound healing as well as sacred ritual and dancing. It has two forks with traverse metal rods that hold small metal disks. Egyptian sistrums are decorated with representations of Hathor.

Sekhmet

Lion-headed goddess of magic and creation, her name means "the most powerful one." When Ra became irritated at humanity and set Sekhmet upon them, she started devouring people with a bloodthirsty fervor. She was eventually offered red-colored beer to drink, which caused her to become intoxicated and stopped the slaughter. As a form of Hathor, she wears a red dress and a sun disk headdress topped by a cobra.

Serapeum

A mysterious, ancient, subterranean complex under Saqqara, Egypt which consists of tunnels and large grottoes in which massive, monolithic granite boxes are inexplicably placed. Conventional archeology maintains that the Serapeum is a burial place for sacred bulls, although the evidence for this hypothesis is inconclusive. The methods by which the 70-ton stone boxes were carved and deposited in the Serapeum are unknown.

Shukren

The phonetic pronunciation of "Thank you," in Egyptian Arabic.

Sorcery

The art and knowledge of using Source energy, alchemy, will, and sometimes spiritual assistance to effect so-called "magical" results. The ability to alter the known laws of nature. Egyptian magic "spells" (*heka*) could be used to heal or curse, although today the word sorcery is often feared as a power linked to evil, black magic and witchcraft.

Sothic

Related to the star Sothis (Sirius). The Egyptians used a Sothic calendar, which made a complete cycle through their solar (365 day) calendar after 1,460 years (referred to as a Sothic cycle).

Sphinx

A carving or depiction of a lion-like or dog-like body with the head of a human or a ram. The Great Sphinx of Giza is the most recognized sphinx in Egypt.

Thebes

The ancient name for an area in Egypt that today encompasses Luxor and Karnak.

Unas

Pharaoh Unas was the last king to reign in Egypt's Fifth Dynasty, which lasted from approximately 2,494 to 2,345 BCE King Unas inscribed the Pyramid Texts (later known as The Book of the Dead) in hieroglyphs on the stone walls of his pyramid in Saqqara—the first known time the wisdom was recorded.

Uraeus

Analogous to "enlightenment." An achievement of spiritual or psychic sight. Esoteric activation, and its accompanying abilities. Symbolized by the upright cobra (the serpent goddess Wadjet) coming out of the forehead of prominent Egyptians in art and on headdresses.

Vishnu

One of the principal three deities of Hinduism, who, along with Brahma and Shiva, forms the Hindu trinity. Vishnu is the peace-loving deity of that trinity, the preserver of the world and restorer of dharma and balance. Like Osiris, Vishnu is a gentle god who is depicted with blue skin.

Younger Dryas

A cataclysmic period between roughly 12,900 and 11,600 years ago that occurred in the Northern Hemisphere at the end of the Pleistocene Epoch. Characterized by extreme temperature changes, multiple catastrophic comet impacts, and a worldwide deluge. Emerging evidence points to a sophisticated—perhaps even technological—prehistoric culture on earth that was destroyed or submerged during the Younger Dryas.

About the Author

Callan Kane is a spiritual explorer, world traveler, and creatrix with a fearless determination to pursue her passions. She founded and published *COWGIRL* magazine for nearly a decade. Her other successes include being a professional writer, Master Falconer, bellydance teacher, competitive surfer, single mother, and accomplished horsewoman. Her name means "Powerful in Battle". This memoir is her first published book.

For more information or to order additional books visit:
callankane.com

9 798218 100087